THE SUNDAY TIMES

How to Prepare a Business Plan

5TH EDITION

Edward Blackwell

KOGAN
PAGE

London and Philadelphia

Throughout the book 'he' and 'she' are used liberally. If there is a preponderance of the male pronoun it is because the inadequacies of the English language do not provide a single personal pronoun suitable to refer to both sexes.

Publisher's note
Every possible effort has been made to ensure that the information contained in this book is accurate at the time of going to press, and the publishers and authors cannot accept responsibility for any errors or omissions, however caused. No responsibility for loss or damage occasioned to any person acting, or refraining from action, as a result of the material in this publication can be accepted by the editor, the publisher or any of the authors.

First published in 1989, reprinted 1989
Second edition 1993, reprinted 1994, reprinted with revisions 1996
Third edition 1998, reprinted 1998
Fourth edition 2002, reprinted 2002, 2003, reprinted with revisions 2004, reprinted 2006
Fifth edition 2008

120 Pentonville Road
London N1 9JN
United Kingdom
www.kogan-page.co.uk

© Edward Blackwell, 2008

The Library
University College for the Creative Arts
at Epsom and Farnham

British Library Cataloguing in Publication Data

A CIP record for this book is available from the British Library.

ISBN 978 0 7494 4981 0

Typeset by Jean Cussons Typesetting, Diss, Norfolk
Printed and bound in India by Replika Press Pvt Ltd

Contents

Acknowledgements

In preparing *How to Prepare a Business Plan*, I have had even more help from my old friend Richard Hughes, FCA, of Edwards Chartered Accountants, Walsall. He has been through the text to make sure, as far as possible, that all the information that needed to be updated has been updated. His advice has always been invaluable.

I have also relied very much on the advice and criticism of Steve Wakefield, who has himself demonstrated how to make a success of catering in an imaginative way.

Throughout the history of the book my wife, Hildegard, has been arbiter and amender of the English, the spelling and the punctuation. Without her the book would never have got off the ground. I also remember with gratitude all my old colleagues who have helped me with so much in the past.

Edward Blackwell

Introduction

Starting a new business venture is like going into a tropical forest on a treasure hunt. There are rewards to be won, in both material wealth and in personal satisfaction, but there are dangers lurking and you can easily lose your way.

This book is written not only to help you convince your financial backers that you will succeed and come back with a bag of gold, but also to help you write your own guidebook for the journey. The author has himself spent 40 years on foot among the trees, both in small business on his own account and as a guide and adviser to others.

Before beginning work on your business plan or your cash flow forecast, you would do well to ask yourself two vital questions.

What do you really want out of the business?

The answer to this question will fall into two parts. The monetary rewards are obviously important. Set yourself a target. If anything less than a million pounds would be a bitter disappointment, then a million is what you are aiming for. If anything above £250 a week would give you cause for a major celebration, put that down as your target.

However, money is not all you are in business for. What else? Are you a born 'loner', anxious to be free from the constraints of a company set-up? Or someone with a yen to organize their own well-structured corporation? Would freedom to design your own products make your life worth living? Or do you just want to feel useful? Your strategy should reflect your own personal ends.

Think, too, about the timescale. Are you determined to make a quick fortune and retire to *la dolce vita* or to a life of good works? Or conversely, are you so fascinated by some aspects of what other people call 'work' that you would happily carry on as long as there is breath in your body?

Just jotting down what you hope to achieve will have begun to give shape to your plan. Next you must ask yourself questions about your resources, both mental and material. Consider your temperament and the talents you will bring to the business, and how they will affect your planning.

Are you an outgoing sort of person, able to get on with and influence your fellow men and women? If so, the marketing side of business – finding out what people want and selling it to them – is likely to be your strong suit; but with that same temperament, you may find you are not very happy or at your most efficient alone in an office and working out costs or struggling with the books. You may not possess, either, the toughness required to deal with employees who do not perform. You might decide, therefore, against trying to run a production-led business or saddling yourself with the bookkeeping.

If you are the creative type but shy and inclined to worry, you would do well to base your business on design and innovation. Having to sell the goods yourself would doubtless prove a trial, and the problems of a production line, controlling the stock and so on, could give you more sleepless nights than you would care to contemplate. Can you make a living by selling your designs and inventions? If so, then concentrate on exploiting your undoubted talents to that end.

In classical times the entrance to the temple of Apollo at Delphi carried the inscription 'Know yourself'. This admonition should be taken to heart by every business man and woman. Others may live happily with illusions about themselves; the small business man or woman cannot!

The primary material resource you will want is of course money. Whether you need a few hundred pounds to start in business as a second-hand clothes dealer or £100,000 to set up a factory, it just has to be there, and a good deal of it must be yours. In the very small business, a rough rule of thumb is that you (or your family and friends) will have to produce half; and the other half is often very hard to come by. I believe that your chances of raising the extra finance will be greatly improved if your business plan and cash-flow forecast are prepared along the lines laid down in this book.

What feature of your product or service will give you the all-important edge over your competitors?

Is your product or service:

- an entirely new idea?
- an improved version of something that already exists?
- cheaper than the others?
- more reliable in delivery or after-sales service?
- more readily available to local customers?
- suitable for sale on the internet?

In writing your plan, both for your own guidance and to reassure your financial backers, you must show that your personal objectives and your resources (both mental and material) are in accord with the strategy you will adopt to exploit the particular feature of your product. This harmony is a major key to success, and careful planning will help you to achieve it.

In this book I have not been content simply to write a set of rules and precepts. I have included several examples of business plans and cash flow forecasts. None of these is to be regarded as an ideal. They represent types or patterns that I consider appropriate and acceptable in each case for the size and type of business under consideration. I do not claim that the facts on which they are based are reliable, but I hope the way in which the imaginary writers of the plans have outlined their sometimes fanciful schemes will prove amusing as well as instructive.

1

Writing a business plan

Business plans are required whenever money is to be raised, whether from a bank, a finance house, or a provider of equity capital. To you, your business is of supreme interest and importance; to the bank or fund manager, your plan is but one of many that are received. So you must win this person's approval and keep his or her interest. To do this:

- be clear;
- be brief;
- be logical;
- be truthful;
- back up words with figures wherever possible.

Clarity

The person reading your business plan is busy, often has other problems to deal with, and is consciously or unconsciously judging you by the way in which you express yourself. Therefore:

- keep your language simple;
- avoid trying to get too many ideas into one sentence;
- let one sentence follow on logically from the last;
- go easy on the adjectives;
- tabulate wherever appropriate.

Brevity

If the banker or manager gets bored while reading your stuff, you are unlikely to get the sympathetic hearing you deserve. So prune and prune again, leaving only the essentials of what your reader ought to be told. In-depth descriptions are out.

Logic

The facts and ideas you present will be easier to take in and make more impact if they follow one another in a logical sequence. Avoid a series of inconsequential paragraphs, however well phrased. Also, make sure that what you say under one heading chimes in with all you have said elsewhere.

Truth

Don't overstate your case.

Figures

The banker or investor reading your plan is numerate, thinking in terms of numbers. Words will not impress a banker unless they are backed by figures that you have made as precise as possible. So try to quantify wherever you can.

Designing the business plan

The layout of your business plan can help greatly in keeping the reader interested. Above all, the information you give must follow a logical pattern. You could present your material in the sequence shown here, using headings, so that the reader can survey your plan and navigate without difficulty.

1. A brief statement of your objectives.
2. Your assessment of the market you plan to enter.
3. The skill, experience and finance you will bring to it.

4. The particular benefits of the product or service to your customers.
5. How you will set up the business.
6. The longer-term view.
7. Your financial targets.
8. The money you are asking for and how it will be used.
9. Appendices to back up previous statements, including especially the cash flow and other financial projections.
10. History of the business (where applicable).

This list can be added to, of course, if the people who will read your business plan have a special interest to which you should address yourself. For instance, public authorities are concerned to know the effect on local unemployment: write a special and prominent section to tell them about it.

Deciding how much to write

In all business plans something, however brief, should be noted on each of the items listed above. How much you put into each section should be in proportion to the size and scope of your project as readers of your plan will see it. Busy bank officials will not want to read through pages of material if they are being asked for no more than a few hundred pounds. On the other hand, they will not be impressed if, when asked to lend £500,000, they are given only a sentence or two on the aspect that interests them most.

Getting down to it

Careful writing of your business plan will give you a better insight into your own business. You have a marvellous project; you have a shrewd idea that there is a market for it; you have obtained a good deal of advice from experts and have done sums to calculate your hoped-for profits, your cash flow and the money you need to raise. So, when you get the finance, you will be ready to go. Or so you believe! But it is odds-on you still have homework to do. Now is the time to do it.

'Writing,' said Sir Francis Bacon, 'makes an exact man.' There is nothing so effective in testing the logic and coherence of your ideas as writing them out – in full. As the future of your business depends in large part on your ideas working in a logical and coherent way, now is the time to subject them to this test.

How to set about it

Taking the numbered sections above one by one, make notes under each heading of all you have done or expect to do. For example, regarding Section 2, what do you really know about the market you want to enter? Have you done enough market research? Who will be your customers? How many will there be? How will you contact them? How will you get your goods to them? When it comes to Section 5, have you a clear, concrete picture of what you will actually do to 'get the show on the road'?

Write it all out! Perhaps you would like to adopt the following method: taking a large sheet of paper for each of the above sections, note down the facts relevant to each of them; then sort them, test for truth and coherence and arrange into a logical pattern.

You will prune hard when you come to write the document itself. In the meantime you will have organized your ideas, you will have noticed gaps and weaknesses, and the business is bound to go the better for it.

Tackling each section

The brief statement

This should be to the point, just something to show the reader what it is all about. Say what you do in one sentence. In a second sentence, state how much money you want and what you want it for.

The market

When you come to the main body of your document, start with the section that is most likely to impress your reader. The majority of people lending money believe that what makes for success in business is finding and exploiting a large enough market. So, as a rule, the 'market' section should be the one with which you lead off.

Although your product may be the best since the invention of the motor car, and you may have the talents of a Henry Ford, you will get nowhere if there is no call for your brainchild or you lack the means of projecting your product into the market. The person reading your plan will know this only too well, and will want to find out whether you are aware of these facts and how well you have done your homework. Your market research is crucial.

Note that where figures are given, and they should be given freely, the authority for the figures should be quoted. If your figures can be checked, this will promote confidence.

The skills, experience and resources of the persons involved

A lender or investor will want to know the track record of the persons to whom his or her own or clients' money is to be entrusted. Therefore, you must give a fairly full account of your own business career and those of your co-directors or partners. School and academic histories are hardly relevant. Past achievements and technical qualifications, on the other hand, are.

Of almost equal importance is the degree of your financial investment. You cannot expect others to risk money in an enterprise to which the founders themselves are not financially committed in a big way.

The benefits of your product

This is the most difficult part about which to comment because it is the section in which you are likely to wax most enthusiastic. Human progress depends on new ideas, and people with good ones need all the support they can get. That having been said, you must face the fact that only a minority of innovations can be made commercially viable. Your banker or financier has probably seen hundreds of absolutely brilliant ideas come to nought, and for all kinds of reasons. So this is the section you will have to write most soberly.

A famous American writer, Ralph Waldo Emerson – a writer, not a businessman – once said that if you made a better mousetrap, all the world would beat a path to your door. This is just not true. Any successful business person could have told Emerson that simply making a better product is only one step on the way to success, and not even the first or the most important step.

Do not get too disheartened. You have, you believe, a first-class product, and as you demonstrated (under number 2 above), the market for it is there. What you must do now is to persuade your reader that your product is a good one and that it will have the edge to help you exploit the opportunities set out in 'the market' above.

Stick firmly to hard facts! 'Puff' sentences, such as 'This is the best widget-grinder on the market and will be the cheapest too', cut very little ice. Show, with figures, why it is the best and why, despite this, it is not the most expensive.

If you have some independent test results, say so, and give at least a summary of them in an appendix. A few genuine figures are worth a page of adjectives, on which, as was stated earlier, you must go easy.

Information that could be included in this section is:

- a brief description of the product or idea;
- how it works;
- why it is better than its rivals;
- any independent appraisal (with details in an appendix).

The method

By this time your reader will have a clear idea of your market, your skills and the customer benefits of your product. What he or she wants to know now is whether you are going to set about things in a sensible and workmanlike manner. Tell your reader what he or she should know in terms that are as concrete as possible.

- First of all, how do you propose to market the product or service? Will you have your own sales force? What will you do about publicity and advertising? How will you 'target' your sales drive? Under what terms will you sell? When will you be starting on all this? Give a firm time schedule, if possible.
- It will promote confidence if you outline your 'management structure'. If you have partners or colleagues, who will be responsible for what? How do you intend to keep the various sections in touch with one another? Will you have management meetings once a week, once a month, or only when there is a desperate crisis? What about keeping employees abreast of what is going on and what is expected of them?
- Outline the production methods you will adopt at the start of the project. Write something, briefly, about the premises you will use. A sentence, or possibly two, will tell of the plant and machinery. You may need a work-force. State how many people you will need at the beginning, and later, as sales increase. What will be the capacity of the initial set-up?
- The office is your next concern. As a skilled engineer or a keen sales-person, you may be impatient of all the paperwork. However, to convince your reader that your business will not descend into chaos or grind to a halt, tell him or her who will see to it that it does not. Who will make sure that the letters are answered in your absence? Who will look after the books? Answer the phone? Process orders? Invoices? Who will chase up

debtors? Have you assessed the amount of work that will need to be done in this department?

■ Your reader will also want to know how you will control and monitor the business financially. The smallest business needs to know at all times what its cash position is. As soon as there are those who owe you money, or to whom you owe money, it will be necessary to keep a regular check. Your banker or investor will know that many an otherwise good business has come to grief through lack of elementary financial controls. Larger businesses will need more elaborate controls. Ensure not only that you have made the necessary arrangements, but that your investor knows you have given this aspect proper regard. Any good accountant should be happy to advise you. This very important point has a whole chapter devoted to it later in the book.

The long-term view

So far, so good. You have explained how you will get your project off the ground and how it will run during the start-up period. Now the banker or investor will want to know how he or she stands for the future.

Some enterprises are essentially short term. Some should continue to be very profitable over a longer period. Some will be slow-growing, and their financial needs can be met out of profits. Others will have to accelerate fast, and they will need further injections of capital on a pre-planned basis. Your financial backer will want to know your thoughts on all these points.

If yours is a project to exploit some 'trendy' idea, the backer will expect some assurance that, if the fashion were to change, he or she could be paid out of ready money and not be locked into un-amortized fixed assets: that is, fixed assets whose cost has not yet been recovered out of profits and which would be difficult to sell. In general, the backer should be told how you see the market over two years, over five years, and in the long term. Also, what you propose to do about potential competition.

The hope is that you will be highly successful. This may well mean that, sooner or later, despite excellent profits, you will need more capital. Here is where you show that you are prepared for this.

Sales forecasts for new ventures are very difficult to make. Trying to predict sales for more than a year ahead is even more difficult, and the experts themselves almost always get it wrong. Usually, such is human nature, they are over-optimistic. But this is no reason for not making the best estimate you can. You need some target on which to base your plans.

In this section you can also write about any developments, new products or new markets – in which you hope to involve your company in the future.

Financial targets

Although your hopes and plans for financing your business will be set out in all the cash flow forecasts and the like, which you will attach as appendices, it will be helpful if you give a brief summary now of the important points. No matter how small the business, you will be expected to show:

- the expected turnover for the first year;
- the expected net profit for the first year;
- how much of the loan will be paid off in one year;
- when you expect to pay off the loan entirely;
- what you hope for in the second year (when payments from the Business Start-up Allowance, if any, will no longer be coming in).

You do not have to show that the business will make a profit in the first year. Your banker knows that many businesses make a loss initially and still go on to succeed. If you show that you can expect to achieve profitability in the long term, your banker should be prepared to go along with this.

However, if you are raising equity capital (see page 121), there are other considerations. Most equity investors expect to be with you a long time. They are interested in capital gain and, if available, dividends. The additional information they will want is:

- the rate at which you expect profits to grow;
- what your dividend policy will be;
- what you and the other directors will be taking out of the business before the equity holders' share in the profits;
- what plans or ambitions you have (if any) to sell out, to buy them out, or to go on the AIM (Alternative Investment Market), a junior branch of the Stock Exchange.

A typical cash flow forecast form as supplied by Barclays Bank is shown on pages 14 to 15. Some of the items listed may not apply in your case, and there may be items missing which you would wish to include. Just delete or leave out non-relevant items and substitute those you want.

Use of the funds

Now that your reader knows that you have a good product, that there is a market for it, and that you know how to run the business in an efficient way, you should explain, in fair detail, why you need his or her money and how you will spend it.

Emphasize how much money you and your colleagues are investing. No one is going to risk money on your project if you are not substantially committed. Having added up the sums you are putting in and all that you are hoping to raise, list the items you will be spending the money on, such as:

- patents;
- land and buildings (give some details);
- plant and equipment (specify major items);
- cost of publicity for the initial launch;
- working capital (reference to cash flow forecasts);
- reserve for contingencies.

The appendices

What you have said so far should have told your reader all about your project. You must now add documentation to convince him or her that you have done your homework properly and that you can show good evidence for what you have said. Last and most important will be the detailed financial forecast. This will vary from the relatively simple cash flow forecast on a form supplied by your bank to an elaborate 'business model' prepared by a professional accountant.

The financial projections are the real meat of the whole business plan. A great deal of information should be given, especially in the cash flow forecast. Chapter 2 is devoted to this subject.

Other appendices could be copies of any documents that will support what you have said previously. They might include:

- accurate summaries of any market research, either your own or research that has been professionally carried out;
- photocopies of local newspaper articles describing a need for a service you propose to provide; pictures of your product or products;
- copies of your leaflets or other promotional literature;
- the results of any testing of your product, especially if it has been done by an independent organization.

Table 1.1 A typical cash flow forecast, supplied by Barclays Bank

Cash flow forecast for: Month   to

Receipts	Month		Month		Month	
	Budget	**Actual**	**Budget**	**Actual**	**Budget**	**Actual**
Cash sales						
Cash from debtors						
Capital introduced						
Total receipts (a)						
Payments						
Payments to creditors						
Salaries/Wages						
Rent/Rates/Water						
Insurance						
Repairs/Renewals						
Heat/Light/Power						
Postage						
Printing/Stationery						
Transport/Motor expenses						
Telephone						
Professional fees						
Capital payments						
Interest charges						
Other						
VAT payable (refund)						
Total payments (b)						
New cash flow (a – b)						
Opening bank balance						
Closing bank balance						

NB All figures include VAT

Month		Month		Month		Totals	
Budget	Actual	Budget	Actual	Budget	Actual	Budget	Actual

The general outline given so far is intended as a guide for those seeking funds for a new enterprise. If you want finance to expand an existing business or to take over an existing shop, the principles will remain the same, but you will need to write an additional paragraph or page, preferably at the beginning of your business plan, to do with the history of the business.

The history of the business

This section should be brief, factual, and based on the audited trading results. At least three years' results should be shown, if possible, as well as the last balance sheet. Reference may be made to such fuller comment, explanation and plans for change as may be given in later pages, such as under 'Marketing' or 'Management'. The history should also tell of any major changes in ownership or management of significant market alterations or trends – in other words, it should mention any important happening that has affected the business over the past few years.

2

Simple cash flow forecasts

What is a cash flow forecast? To those who are venturing into business for the first time, the prospect of having to draw up a cash flow forecast can be intimidating; but the banks will demand one when a loan is sought for even the smallest of one-person enterprises. This is because banks believe it will give them at least some idea whether and when they are likely to get their money back.

The cash flow forecast sets out, usually in monthly columns, the sums you expect to receive by way of sales, Business Start-up Allowance etc, and compares this inflow of money with the payments you will be making for stock, materials, overheads, equipment, and the money you will have to take out of the business for living expenses. An example is shown on pages 14 to 15.

It is not a forecast of the profitability of the business, but merely a guess as to whether, in the short term, more cash will come in than go out. That is not necessarily the same as profitability. On the one hand, although your profit margins might not be adequate to cover overheads and write off the cost of equipment, your cash flow could be good enough to pay the bank back its money while you are losing your own.

On the other hand, there are profitable businesses (ones where the net assets are growing nicely) that are what is called 'cash hungry'. They may be making fine profits, but all the cash they take in, and more, is needed to increase stock or give credit to an ever larger number of customers. So the bank, far from getting its money back, will be lending more and more. Sooner or later the bank will call a halt, and the business may have to close, despite its underlying profitability.

Is a cash flow forecast of any real use?

A cash flow forecast that is badly drawn up is clearly of little use. It serves merely as a snare and a delusion. Unfortunately, the project figures in your forecast will depend on the reliability of your crystal ball in foretelling your sales figures. You may improve the accuracy of those figures by conscientious market research or by getting advance orders (or at least firm promises), but you will still be peering into an uncertain future.

However, if the sales figures appear reasonable and conservative, and if the cash flow forecast has been well and logically drawn up, the bank will be able to take a view as to whether it can lend the money (and get it back again without having to sell up your house and furniture – a step even the toughest bank manager is loath to take).

To persuade the bank or building society to lend you the money you need is, of course, the primary purpose of a cash flow forecast. It has, however, some other very important uses.

Actually producing a well-thought-out forecast fulfils the same function as writing a well-prepared business plan. It will sharpen up your ideas. It will make you aware of the effect on your bank balance of the decisions you take in your planning, such as the amounts to be spent on advertising, your terms of sale (very important for cash flow), whether or not to buy your own transport and so on. Giving thought to your cash flow is a very worthwhile exercise. Try drawing up several forecasts, each based on rather different assumptions of sales and expenditure. The few hours you spend could prove the most profitable of your life!

Even the smallest business is more likely to do well if its owner keeps a close eye on its financial progress, comparing what is hoped and planned for with what is actually happening. In business jargon this is called 'budgetary control'. In your cash flow forecast you will have an invaluable little tool when you come to set up your own small-scale budgetary control. So don't tear it up once the bank has seen it. Use it. Most of the banks appreciate the value of their cash flow sheets as budgetary control documents, and provide adjoining columns for 'forecast' and 'actual'. If, every month and immediately after the month-end, you fill in all the figures in the 'actual' column, you will get a quick indication of anything that is going wrong, together with strong hints about where to target any remedial action.

Principles to observe when filling in a simple cash flow form

1. Enter the more certain figures first.
2. Make every entry in the month in which cash and cheques are handed over.
3. All entries must be inclusive of VAT where applicable.

Start by entering those payments of which you are certain (or almost certain):

- the rent – in the actual months when it must be paid;
- the rates – for each month when they must be paid;
- HP payments on any vehicles or machinery;
- loan repayments on any fixed-term loan you have agreed or hope to agree;
- wages of any regular employees;
- the sums you will have to draw from the business to live on;
- any other payments you expect to have to make if you know the amounts.

Now also enter the sure regular receipts, such as:

- Business Start-up Allowance payments;
- rents from any sub-let.

The next items are more difficult. They are overhead payments, the amounts of which are not yet certain because the invoices have not been received. These will include:

- gas and electricity bills;
- telephone bills;
- advertising and publicity costs;
- petrol and other motor expenses;
- stationery and printing;
- postage and packaging;
- insurance premiums;
- repairs and renewals;
- etc (the etceteras will depend on the nature of your business).

These items cannot be predicted with any great accuracy, but if you have done your homework, you should be able to make reasonable estimates. Enter them, of course, for the months when you will have to pay them. 'Repairs and renewals' are a special case. They are by their very nature uncertain, in both amount and timing. Make a good guess about the yearly cost and divide this into four quarterly payments.

The next thing to do is to enter the initial receipts and payments – those once-and-for-all transactions that get you started. The receipts could include:

- fixed loans from the bank;
- loans from family or friends;
- money of your own which you pay into the business account after the date of start-up;
- grants.

The payments could include:

- capital payments for the lease;
- machinery and equipment;
- initial licence fees;
- legal fees;
- installation costs;
- office equipment;
- starting stock;
- advertising to launch the product.

Remember that the cash flow forecast is deemed to start on a specific day – usually the first of the month. Any payments made or moneys received before that date must be ignored. You are writing a cash flow, not a profit and loss account.

Many of these initial costs will be paid in the first month and should be entered in the appropriate spaces for that month. However, you may get extended credit for, say, 30 days or six weeks for some items. Enter them for the months in which they will actually be paid.

Most of your figures will have been entered now. But you will still have the difficult part to do. You must tackle the sales side. This is a matter of putting hard figures to the faith you have in your product. You know in your bones that the product or service will sell. But how well? And how soon will the money start to come in? You will have done some market research even if, as a potential window cleaner, you have done nothing more than call on the neighbours to find out how many will pay to have their windows cleaned. Use all the information you have gleaned about your market; link this with the amount of time you will be able to devote to selling, and you should be able to make some sort of educated guess at the turnover you can expect once you have got going properly.

Your sales will certainly not be the same month by month. For one thing, you will probably take a month or two to reach the sales target you have set yourself. Adjust your figures to allow for this possible slow build-up.

Pre-start orders from friends or from business contacts will give you a splendid start and help enormously with the cash flow for the first month or two, but they are easy orders, and there may well be a downturn in later months when you have to start relying on new sales to new contacts.

Now you may not be in the business of making chocolate Easter eggs or Mother's Day bouquets, but there is almost certain to be some seasonal element in your business. It may be nothing more than that you, as a self-employed worker, go away for an annual holiday. But build this seasonal factor into the sales profile.

If yours is a 'cash only' business, you can enter your monthly sales figures straight on the 'cash sales' line on the chart. But, if you are going to give credit to your customers, the cash flow will have to be adjusted for this. That share of the sales that is for cash (or cheques) will still be entered on the 'cash sales' line, but the credit sales will suffer a time lag before they are entered on the 'cash from debtors' line. This time-lag will depend on two factors: your 'terms of sale' as regards time allowed for payment, and your customers' adherence to those terms. Incidentally, do make sure that your terms of sale are stated clearly on your quotations. Simply putting them on your invoice has no legally binding force.

If your terms of sale decree payment in 30 days and half your customers observe them, then you will receive payment for 50 per cent of this month's credit sales next month and 50 per cent in the month after next. Likewise, if you give 60 days' credit and two-thirds pay within the time given them, you will get payment for 66 per cent of this month's sales the month after next, and 33 per cent in three months' time.

There is also the question of the discount you offer in order to obtain prompt payment. This too affects the cash flow.

There are innumerable variations of both simple and sophisticated trade terms that can be offered. You will adopt the ones that suit your market best, but with the strong proviso that only the cash-rich can afford to give credit without offering discounts for prompt payment.

Let us take some examples, assuming monthly sales of £1,000 per month. See Tables 2.1 to 2.4.

Table 2.1 Terms – net 30 days (half pay on time)

	May £	June £	July £	August £
May sales paid	0	500	500	
June sales paid		0	500	500
July sales paid				500
Totals	0	500	1,000	1,000

Table 2.2 Terms – same, but given 2½ per cent discount for immediate payment (half take the discount, the rest split as before)

	May £	June £	July £	August £
May sales paid	487	250	250	
June sales paid		487	250	250
July sales paid			487	250
August sales paid				487
Totals	487	737	987	987

Table 2.3 Terms – 60 days' credit, no discount (two-thirds pay on time)

	May £	June £	July £	August £
May sales paid	0	0	667	333
June sales paid		0	0	667
July sales paid			0	0
Totals	0	0	667	1000

Table 2.4   Terms – same as for Table 2.3, but 5 per cent discount given for immediate payment (half take the discount, the rest split as before)

	May £	**June** £	**July** £	**August** £
May sales paid	475	0	333	167
June sales paid		475	0	333
July sales paid			475	0
August sales paid				475
Totals	475	475	808	975

You have now settled the cash sales line and the 'receipts from debtors'. The time has come to settle the purchase of 'materials' (or 'goods for resale', as the case may be). You are going to run a tight ship, of course, as far as purchases are concerned. You have seen too many businesses go down the river through bad buying. You will avoid, therefore, buying more than you need for current production or sales, however tempting the bulk purchase discount. Excellent!

So your purchases will be strictly related to your sales figures. As far as possible you will buy in the month what you will use – or sell – in the month. If you are in a trading business (exceptions will be dealt with below), your purchases for the month will equal your sales, less the average mark-up. If yours is a manufacturing business, you must take into consideration the 'lead time of production', that is to say, the actual time it takes to make the goods up to the time of invoicing them, and your purchases must be adjusted accordingly.

Let us deal with the retail or pure trading business first. Here, to the best of your ability, you are buying to sell in the same month. So the purchases will equal the sales, less the average trade discount. If you have to pay cash for goods, that is that. But very likely, you can get at least a month's credit from suppliers, so sales will lead purchases.

Let us take some examples, assuming in all cases a mark-up of 33.3 per cent on selling price.

This pattern of payments and receipts, which is by no means uncommon, is worth a little study. Note the sudden cash shortage that appears in August and January. These are the months in which heavy payments are made, and especially in August, the cash receipts are relatively low. If money is not held back from, say, July or December to meet the requirements of August and January, the business could well be in difficulties. Any self-employed person should keep a cash flow forecast and update it regularly just to watch out for such problems.

Table 2.5 All sales for cash. All purchases for cash. Sales a steady £5,000 per month, except in August and December

	May £	June £	July £	Aug £	Sept £	Oct £	Nov £	Dec £	Jan £
Cash sales	5,000	5,000	5,000	2,500	5,000	5,000	5,000	10,000	5,000
Purchases	3,333	3,333	3,333	1,666	3,333	3,333	3,333	6,666	3,333
Cash flow	1,667	1,667	1,667	834	1,667	1,667	1,667	3,334	1,667

Table 2.6 As before, but 30 days' credit is received for half the purchases

	May £	June £	July £	Aug £	Sept £	Oct £	Nov £	Dec £	Jan £
Cash sales	5,000	5,000	5,000	2,500	5,000	5,000	5,000	10,000	5,000
Purchase payments									
for this month	1,667	1,666	1,666	833	1,667	1,667	1,667	3,333	1,667
for last month	0	1,667	1,667	1,667	833	1,666	1,666	1,666	3,333
Payments to creditors	1,667	3,333	3,333	2,500	2,500	3,333	3,333	4,999	5,000
Cash flow	3,333	1,667	1,667	0	2,500	1,667	1,667	5,001	0

Let us return to our examples. It is interesting to see, in Table 2.7, that the month of highest sales produces one of the lowest cash flows, whereas the month of lowest sales produces the second-highest cash flow. This is by no means an unusual phenomenon.

The choice of trade terms can seriously affect your cash flow, not only in your paper forecasts but for deadly earnest in real life. You will have to decide what are the best terms, appropriate to your situation for both buying and selling, that you can reasonably expect to obtain; then apply them to your cash flow forecast.

It is assumed that you will be able to relate your purchases to sales on a month to month basis, as should be possible in most cases. However, when there is an element of 'fashion' involved, this close relationship between sales and purchases does not apply.

For example, in the dress or shoe trade, there are summer styles and winter styles. All buying for the summer is done in the winter for delivery and invoicing in, say, March/April. A similar time-lag applies to the winter trade. In this type of business, what is not sold in one season is unlikely to be worth hanging

Table 2.7   As Table 2.5, but half the sales are on 30 days' credit and half the customers pay on time

	May £	June £	July £	Aug £	Sept £	Oct £	Nov £	Dec £	Jan £
Total sales	5,000	5,000	5,000	2,500	5,000	5,000	5,000	10,000	5,000
Credit sales	2,500	2,500	2,500	1,250	2,500	2,500	2,500	5,000	2,500
Cash from debtors									
last month's		1,250	1,250	1,250	625	1,250	1,250	1,250	2,500
two months ago			1,250	1,250	1,250	625	1,250	1,250	1,250
Cash sales	2,500	2,500	2,500	1,250	2,500	2,500	2,500	5,000	2,500
Total cash received	2,500	3,750	5,000	3,750	4,375	4,375	5,000	7,500	6,250
Payments to creditors	3,333	3,333	3,333	1,666	3,333	3,333	3,333	6,666	3,333
Cash flow	−833	417	1,667	2,084	1,042	1,042	1,667	834	2,917

on to for the next-but-one. Hence the end-of-season sales, when goods are sold for whatever they will fetch, sometimes for less than cost. Anything that could become dead stock must be turned into cash quickly at almost any price.

Let us take, for example, a firm that buys £80,000 worth of goods during the year, evenly split between summer and winter. The mark-up on cost is 100 per cent. The firm expects to sell 85 per cent during the season, the remainder to go into the seasonal sales at cost. The cash pattern will be that shown in Table 2.8.

Table 2.8   Cash pattern example

	Cash received £	Payments £	Cash flow excluding overheads £
April	17,000	40,000	−23,000
May	17,000		17,000
June	17,000		17,000
July	17,000		17,000
August (sales)	16,000		16,000
September	17,000	40,000	−23,000
October	17,000		17,000
November	17,000		17,000
December	17,000		17,000
January (sales)	16,000		16,000

The principle of relating purchases of materials to expected sales also applies to a manufacturing company. Random buying is out. Avoid above all the temptation to buy more than you know you will need in the short term just because of a very favourable discount you are offered.

Your purchases must relate to your production schedule, which in turn must relate to your forecast of sales. Table 2.8 has been highly simplified by taking two seasons of five months each, ignoring February and March, and by assuming that profit-earning sales are spread evenly.

If you have been following my suggestions and filling in the figures on your cash flow forecast, it ought to be nearly complete. Only one or two tidying-up operations remain to be done. The first, but by no means the most important, is to provide a 'contingency fund' or a 'Murphy's Law (if anything can go wrong, it will go wrong) allowance'. It is a provision you would do well to make to cover all those unforeseen misfortunes that crop up to plague the business person. It is not there to cover shortfalls on items for which you have budgeted above, but to protect you, to some extent at least, against the wholly unexpected. Calculate it as a small percentage, perhaps 2.5 per cent of turnover. Treat it as VATable and enter it monthly.

The second and much more important operation is to allow for VAT, if you have registered for it. You have presumably included VAT in the entries you have made so far; it now remains to calculate the quarterly payments you will have to make to the Customs and Excise (or, if applicable, the repayment claims).

You are probably taking advantage of the Finance Act of 1987 and paying VAT on a cash basis. VAT is usually paid quarterly, the month after the end of the quarter. For example, if your last quarter ended on 30 April, then in May you will pay VAT for the months of February, March and April.

You begin by adding up the sales, including VAT for the first three months, multiply by 17.5 and divide by 1.175. This will give you your VAT 'output' tax. Next, you add up the VATable items of expenditure for the same three months and do the same calculation. This gives you your VAT 'input' tax. The difference will be the VAT you will pay in the fourth month.

The following expenses are not VATable:

- rent (in almost all cases – but check with care);
- rates;
- wages and National Insurance;
- insurance, subject to insurance tax;
- bus and train fares;
- bank interest and most charges;

- postage;
- licence fees;
- books etc.

Note, too, that VAT on motor cars (other than vans and lorries, and those used for special business purposes, eg taxis) is not recoverable.

You will remember that in a previous paragraph you were cautioned against including in your cash-flow forecast any expenditure paid for before day one. However, the VAT you have paid as part of such expenditure does come into the calculations because you can recover it, and it will be part of the 'input' tax that you claim for in the first quarter. So the pre-start-up VAT must be added in when you do the first quarter's calculations.

You will calculate in the same way for the second and the third quarters, but the fourth quarter's VAT will not be part of this cash flow forecast. This is because it will not be paid until the first month of the second year (where it will have to appear like any other creditor at the end of the year if you are doing a second-year forecast).

If you are borrowing from the bank, you still have the bank interest to deal with. If, however, you decided that it would be more economical to raise the money by remortgaging your house with your building society, the interest will be taken care of in the repayment arrangements and does not form a separate item. But let us assume that you are borrowing from the bank.

The loan can take one of two forms. It can either be a loan for a fixed term, with fixed repayment arrangements, or it can be in the form of an overdraft facility. In the first case, the loan is sure, the repayments are fixed, and the interest can be calculated readily with reference to the prevailing bank rate. On the other hand, you will have to pay interest on the whole of the outstanding loan even if your current account is well in the black. The overdraft facility, although it has the advantage of only incurring interest on the amount outstanding at any time, is less certain, as the bank can withdraw or reduce it at any time. However, it is particularly appropriate as a means of covering temporary fluctuations in cash flow due to, say, seasonal patterns of buying. Most banks are prepared to negotiate a mixture of fixed loan and overdraft to meet the individual case.

With all the figures for cash in and cash out now entered, you can add up the 'ins' and the 'outs' for each month and work out the effect on your bank balance. Each bank has its own cash flow forecast form, and you will have to do the calculations according to the bank's method. In principle, you start with the current account balance on the day you begin business; you add 'cash in' and take away 'cash out'. Your new end-of-the-month balance, of course, becomes the starting balance for the next month.

Your cash flow forecast is now ready to be pinned to your business plan and handed in to the bank. A cash flow forecast as outlined above is probably as complicated a production as can be expected from someone lacking professional training. It will just about do when a loan of up to £2,000 or £3,000 is wanted. But if tens of thousands of pounds are required, then a more sophisticated document will have to be prepared, preferably a full business model, with forecast profit and loss accounts and balance sheets. This is a task that should be put into the hands of professionally qualified accountants, and is not covered here.

At the end of Chapters 3 and 5, examples are given to demonstrate, step by step, how a simple cash flow forecast is prepared.

The break-even analysis

The cash flow forecast that you have just drawn up is designed to assure a bank manager or other lender that they are likely to get their money back. It is also, as explained above, a fine tool for helping you to understand your business better. Even more useful, however, is what is called a 'break-even analysis' – a means of determining how much you must sell in order to meet your commitments.

To produce a sample break-even analysis:

1. Add up all your overheads and the payments you will have to make whether you produce anything or not. Included will be rent, rates, insurance, lighting and heating, etc; also office staff wages, the basic wages of production workers, interest on bank overdrafts or loans, sales costs and, of course, depreciation.
2. Work out the cost of making one article, excluding all the above overheads, etc. Included in this 'marginal cost', as it is called, will be raw materials, royalties (if any), consumable stores such as packing material, and those wages that are directly related to production: piece work or bonus payments and overtime.
3. Settle on your selling price (which should be the highest your market will stand).
4. Work out the difference between the cost (2) and the selling price to determine your gross profit per unit.
5. Now work out how many units you will have to sell to meet your commitments before you make a penny for yourself.

For example, John Smith's projected overheads are going to be £50,000 per year. His 'marginal cost' per unit is made up as follows:

Materials	200p
Piece-work wages	100p
Packaging, etc	10p
Total	310p

John can sell for £5 per item plus VAT. This means his gross profit per item is £1.90. John must sell 26,316 units (£50,000) every year just to cover his overheads and he must sell 31,579 (approximately 640 per week) if he wants to make a profit of £10,000 for himself.

An analysis like this can, of itself, raise important questions that will have to be answered. How is John going to sell his production? Can he sell to bulk buyers or will he have to employ a sales staff? Paying fixed salaries to sales staff could well increase his overheads by 50 per cent, which in turn would mean selling 50 per cent more just to break even! Perhaps he could find an agent to sell on commission. If so, the commission, though not an overhead (since it is determined by the number sold), is a cost directly adding to the 'marginal cost', thus reducing the gross profit per item and making it necessary to sell more.

You can see how thought-provoking a break-even analysis can be, and how useful it is if properly applied. If, every time the circumstances affecting the business changed in any way, a new cash flow forecast and a new break-even analysis were drawn up, many more small firms and sole traders would avoid bankruptcy.

3

The very small business

If you want to set up a business yourself or go into partnership with a friend, you may wonder why you should go to the trouble of writing a formal business plan. Why not just fill in the bank's own cash flow form and explain all else at an interview?

There are two good reasons why you should write out a proper plan: first, as pointed out in Chapter 1, because it will help you to understand your business and its problems better; and second, because of the nature of bank procedures.

It may be that your bank manager is a friendly type who really wants to help the small business, but he or she will be working under conditions imposed from above – an expensive member of a big bureaucracy. No doubt bank managers would like to be perceived as the benevolent figures portrayed in some TV ads, dispensing advice to all customers. In practice, however, most of the bank manager's time is spent in administration, dealing with the problems of those further down in the bank's hierarchy and reporting to those above. The manager also has to promote and advertise the bank locally, so the amount of time allocated for actually dealing with customers is not unlimited. Naturally enough, the manager is expected to concentrate on the best-paying customers – the bigger ones. One cannot reasonably hope for anything else. The bank is not a charity.

Therefore, except in the smaller branches, it is highly likely that your application for a loan with be dealt with by, in the first instance, a junior, though the manager may make the final decision. Now there are problems in dealing with a junior, even when 'manager' appears as part of his or her title. For one thing, a junior is only given power to say 'No', and will have very limited power to say 'Yes'. Almost certainly the junior's main function is to act as a filter, so that the manager will not have to waste time on doubtful cases. Moreover, this junior status may mean that as yet neither his or her good judgement nor conscientiousness has been proved. Therefore you must spare no effort to ensure that your application goes forward to the real decision maker. A well-written business plan will not only be impressive in itself, it will save the junior having to write up a report on your project. This could give you a big advantage.

Once you have decided to write the plan, you will have to decide how much to say. Facing the fact that the bank will see you as small fry, you will be well advised to limit the main part of the plan to two typed A4 pages, or three at the very most. You can add appendices, such as those listed on page 13, which could include a fuller account of any technical details you feel should be added, and of course the cash flow forecast. You do not have to write as much as if you were starting a larger concern, such as those described in the later chapters.

However, even in a two-page document, you must cover the points listed in Chapter 1, namely:

- what it is all about (often one sentence will do);
- how big your market is and what the competition is;
- if you have already started, what progress has been made;
- your own skill and experience;
- how your product or project compares with others;
- how you will get your act together;
- the longer-term view;
- how much turnover and profit you can expect;
- the money you need and why.

The same principles apply as listed on the first page of Chapter 1. On the following pages you will find examples of business plans appropriate when applying for a loan of a few hundred pounds. I shall also go through the stages of filling out a bank's cash flow forecast form.

Example 3.1: Alexander Battersby

My name is Alexander Battersby. I am a skilled joiner by trade and I wish to borrow £500 to set up in business on my own.

The market for my services

My uncle, George Battersby, who has been a self-employed joiner for

20 years, has decided to retire and will let me have his list of customers and contacts and sell me his tools. In the last year or two he has been doing about £950 worth of work a month. I am sure that, with extra energy, I can increase this to at least £1,200 per month and that will involve less than 20 hours per week actually working on the jobs.

I have also been talking to the managers of two of the local DIY shops. Both tell me that at least one in ten DIY projects started by householders runs into trouble and that many people, having started a job, wish they had never begun. If I advertise myself as being willing to put things right, I am sure I could get a lot of profitable work.

About myself

I am a fully trained joiner, with nine years' experience since completing my apprenticeship.

I have also had experience in plastering and decorating and have some skills in tiling and bricklaying.

I am attending a course in design at the local technical college. I am married with one son.

How I will set about my business

I cannot use my own house as a base, but my Uncle George will let me use his old premises at his house until I can find suitable ones of my own. I will pay him £15 a week rent.

I shall have to buy a van. To do this I will sell my car. I can get a good second-hand van for £1,900, and I will get £900 for my car after paying off the HP.

Advertising in the first month in the local paper will cost £100. To emphasize continuity with my uncle, I will trade as Battersby & Co.

A lady called Doreen Gray runs a bookkeeping and secretarial service. I have been strongly recommended to use her services to keep my paperwork in order. This will cost £100 per month.

I also intend to give written quotations for every job to avoid arguments afterwards. I shall insure against third-party risks.

The future

If the business reaches a turnover of more than £61,000 I shall have to register for VAT. For the present, most of my customers will be private people who will not be able to recover the VAT I should have to charge. My ambition is to get more work from builders and others who are registered for VAT themselves, so that in the long term I will no longer have to rely on private customers.

How I will use the money

I have £1,800 of my own in a building society. I am asking for an overdraft facility of £500. The money will be used as follows:

	£
	£
Van	1,000
Tools	500
Licences and sundries	150
Advertising	100
Working capital	135
Total	1,885

Paying back the money

As will be seen from the enclosed cash flow forecast, I do not expect to use the whole of the overdraft, but I have asked for enough to cover any normal misfortune. I intend to pay back any overdraft within the six-month period, even if the sales are less than expected.

The information given by Alexander leaves some questions unanswered, but it is quite clear that he knows what he is about, and that he has thought over the problems he will face in going it alone. He realized that his knowledge of bookkeeping is limited. If Doreen Gray is even moderately competent, she will keep him clear of the paperwork muddle that defeats so many self-employed people. And on the basis of this plan, most bank managers should look upon Alexander as a good risk for a small loan.

But there is still the cash flow forecast to prepare. Let's go through the steps as they apply to Alexander. For purposes of illustration we shall assume that Alexander Battersby is applying to Barclays Bank for a loan, and in preparing his cash flow forecast, is using the form depicted on pages 14 to 15.

Alexander realizes that certain items on this form will not apply in his case. Alexander will insist on cash payment, so all his sales will be 'cash sales'. He will not have to fill in the 'cash from debtors' line, nor will be he paying any wages yet, so he could use this line for his own drawings.

The lines for 'HP/leasing repayments' and 'VAT' do not apply to his business, as he has no HP debts and is not registered for VAT. So all these lines can be blanked out and used, if needed, for something else.

Now, following the principles laid down in Chapter 2, Alexander will have to fill in the blanks for the certain payments he will be making. They will be:

- Rent/rates – rent, including rates, is payable weekly at £15 per week, ie approximately £60 per month, starting in month one.
- Payments to Doreen Gray – at £100 per month, and as she will be paid each month for the work she did the previous month, the first entry will be made in month two.
- Drawings – Alexander and his family have to live, and he decides he must draw £500 per month from the business, starting in month one.

Many people going into business for the first time ask what wages they can pay themselves on PAYE. This question reveals a misunderstanding on the tax status of someone who is self-employed or running his or her own business as a sole trader or in partnership. Unless you form a limited company, which is usually inadvisable, you cannot pay yourself 'wages' which are subject to PAYE. You will be taxed at the end of the year on the profits you have made, and you cannot affect those profits and the tax payable thereon by paying yourself 'wages' or 'salary'. In fact, the amount of income tax payable will not be affected by how much or how little you draw out of the business for yourself. (You can, however, if your spouse works in the business, pay him or her a wage, and this will be subject to PAYE.)

It is strongly recommended that you keep your business payments and your private or household payments strictly separate. Adopt a system of making regular drawings from the business account, and never pay for private expenditure out of the business directly. In most cases it pays to have two separate bank accounts (or a bank account and a building society account), one for business, the other for private and family use. Keeping the two apart will save you no end of trouble and confusion.

Getting back to Alexander Battersby and his cash flow forecast, there are the other ongoing overheads (as listed in Chapter 2):

- Electricity – Alexander believes he will have to pay his uncle approximately £50 per quarter to cover his share of the bill. Enter for 'heating/light/power'.
- Telephone – Alexander has a telephone at home and estimates that he ought to contribute £50 every quarter from the business account. Enter £50 on the 'telephone' line in March and June. (Alexander must pay these sums into his private account in the designated months.)
- Advertising – it is hoped that the business will grow by word of mouth after advertisement in the local press and a distribution of leaflets that will take place at the start. However, Alexander will budget for £50 every three months starting in May.
- Petrol and other motor expenses – £60 every month, with an extra £200 every quarter to cover oil, repairs, etc.
- Stationery and printing – after the initial expense, £5 per month is expected to cover this.
- Insurance premiums – these are paid in the first month: £300.
- Repairs and renewals – Alexander does not think he will need to spend much on repairs for some time, other than perhaps to the motor van. However, he agrees it would be wise to allow £20 per month to cover 'contingencies'.

You can now see (Table 3.1, page 36) how Alexander's cash flow forecast will look at this stage.

Alexander himself will now have a good idea of what he will need to earn in order to cover his monthly overheads and feed and clothe his family. He reckons his earnings will have to average at least £650 per month.

The next step will be to fill in the start-up payments and receipts. You will remember that Alexander listed his start-up costs. The van and tools – together £1,500 – will be entered as 'capital items' and others as 'licences and sundries'. ('Working capital' is not entered. This item will be dealt with later.)

On the first day of trading Alexander will withdraw the £1,800 from his building society account and pay it into his new business account at the bank. The amount will be entered as 'capital introduced'.

The cash flow forecast will now look like Table 3.2, page 37.

Next, the sales figures must be tackled. The estimate of sales in this case is made relatively simple by the fact that Alexander is sure he can carry on where

Table 3.1 Alexander Battersby's cash flow forecast #1

Cash flow forecast for: A Battersby Month January to June

	Jan		Feb		Mar		Apr		May		June		Totals	
Receipts	Budget	Actual	Budget	Actual	Budget	Actual	Budget	Actual	Budget	Actual	Budget	Actual	Budget	Actual
Cash sales														
Cash from debtors														
Capital introduced														
Total receipts (a)														
Payments														
Payments to creditors														
Salaries/wages														
Rent/rates/water	60		60		60		60		60					
Insurance	300													
Repairs/renewals	20		20		20		20		20					
Heat/light/power					50				50					
Advertising														
Printing/stationery			5		5		5		5					
Transport/motor expenses	60		260		260		60		260					
Telephone					50				50					
Professional fees (D Gray)			100		100		100		100					
Capital payments														
Interest charges														
Drawings	500		500		500		500		500					
VAT payable (refund)														
Total payments (b)														
New cash flow (a–b)														
Opening bank balance														
Closing bank balance														

Table 3.2 Alexander Battersby's cash flow forecast #2
Cash flow forecast for: A Battersby Month January to June

	Jan		Feb		Mar		Apr		May		June		Totals	
	Budget	Actual	Budget	Actual	Budget	Actual	Budget	Actual	Budget	Actual	Budget	Actual	Budget	Actual
Receipts														
Cash sales														
Cash from debtors														
Capital introduced	1800													
Total receipts (a)														
Payments														
Payments to creditors														
Salaries/wages														
Rent/rates/water	60		60		60		60		60					
Insurance	300													
Repairs/renewals	20		20		20		20		20					
Heat/light/power					50				50					
Advertising	100						50							
Printing/stationery			5		5		5		5					
Transport/motor expenses	60		60		260		60		260					
Telephone					50				50					
Professional fees (D Gray)	100		100		100		100		100					
Capital payments	1500													
Interest charges														
Drawings	500		500		500		500		500					
Licences and sundries	150													
Total payments (b)														
New cash flow (a–b)														
Opening bank balance														
Closing bank balance														

Table 3.3 Alexander Battersby's cash flow forecast #3
Cash flow forecast for: A Battersby Month January to June

	Jan Budget	Jan Actual	Feb Budget	Feb Actual	Mar Budget	Mar Actual	Apr Budget	Apr Actual	May Budget	May Actual	June Budget	June Actual	Totals Budget	Totals Actual
Receipts														
Cash sales	750		950		1150		1150		1200		1200		6400	
Cash from debtors														
Capital introduced	1800												1800	
Total receipts (a)	2550		950		1150		1150		1200		1200		8200	
Payments														
Payments to creditors			45		57		69		69		72		312	
Cash purchases	45		57		69		69		72		72		384	
Rent/rates/water	60		60		60		60		60		60		360	
Insurance	300												300	
Repairs/renewals	20		20		20		20		20		20		120	
Heat/light/power					50						50		100	
Advertising	100								50				150	
Printing/stationery			5		5		5		5		5		25	
Transport/motor expenses	60		60		260		60		60		260		760	
Telephone					50						50		100	
Professional fees (D Gray)			100		100		100		100		100		500	
Capital payments	1500												1500	
Interest charges														
Drawings	500		500		500		500		500		500		3000	
Licences and sundries	150												150	
Total payments (b)	2735		847		1171		883		936		1189		7761	
New cash flow (a–b)														
Opening bank balance														
Closing bank balance														

Table 3.4 Alexander Battersby's cash flow forecast #4

Cash flow forecast for: A Battersby Month January to June

Receipts	Month Jan		Month Feb		Month Mar		Month Apr		Month May		Month June		Totals	
	Budget	Actual	Budget	Actual	Budget	Actual	Budget	Actual	Budget	Actual	Budget	Actual	Budget	Actual
Cash sales	750		950		1150		1150		1200		1200		6400	
Cash from debtors														
Capital introduced	1800												1800	
Total receipts (a)	2550		950		1150		1150		1200		1200		8200	
Payments														
Payments to creditors			45		57		69		69		72		312	
Cash purchases	45		57		69		69		72		72		384	
Rent/rates/water	60		60		60		60		60		60		360	
Insurance	300												300	
Repairs/renewals	20		20		20		20		20		20		120	
Heat/light/power					50						50		100	
Advertising	100								50				150	
Printing/stationery			5		5		5		5		5		25	
Transport/motor expenses	60		60		260		60		60		260		760	
Telephone					50						50		100	
Professional fees (D Gray)			100		100		100		100		100		500	
Capital payments	1500												1500	
Interest charges							35						35	
Drawings	500		500		500		500		500		500		3000	
Licences and sundries	150												150	
Total payments (b)	2735		847		1171		918		936		1189		7796	
New cash flow (a–b)	–185		103		–21		232		264		11			
Opening bank balance	Nil		–185		–82		–103		129		393			
Closing bank balance	–185		–82		–103		129		393		404			

NB: All figures include VAT

his uncle left off – with basic sales of £850. In the first month the sales figure will be less, however, because he will not have been able to finish a biggish job and will not, therefore, be paid for it until later. Alexander believes that by April his sales campaign – leaflets and personal visits – will have paid off and his sales increased. The cash sales, he hopes, will be:

January	February	March	April	May	June
£750	£950	£1,050	£1,500	£1,200	£1,200

These figures are entered on the 'cash sales' line.

Next, the purchase of materials must be dealt with. Alexander estimates that the cost of materials will account for about 12 per cent of the amount charged on bills sent out, as a good deal of his work will consist of repairs. At a turnover of £750, this works out at £90.

Uncle George has arranged with some of his suppliers to continue to extend a month's credit on supplies when Alexander takes over. Half Alexander's materials will be obtainable on this basis. So his 'cash purchases' line will look like this:

January	February	March	April	May	June
£45	£57	£69	£69	£72	£72

The 'payments to creditors' line will show:

0	£45	£57	£69	£69	£72

Now Alexander has nearly completed his cash flow forecast and can add up the columns and rows – preferably in pencil at this stage. The sheet should look like Table 3.3 (page 38).

The bank balance lines remain to be filled in. As Alexander is starting at 9 am on day one with nothing in the bank – his own £1,800 to be paid in later that day – he enters 'nil' as his opening balance and works out the closing balance as instructed on Barclays' form. He finds he will be overdrawn by £185 at the month end, and this is the figure he uses as 'working capital' in the business plan paragraphs above.

The closing bank balance for one month becomes the opening bank balance for the next month, so Alexander will only need one more item to complete the form. The bank official has told him what the standard bank charges will be, and Alexander realizes that there will be interest for two months. A quick calculation shows him that his bank charges and interest for the first quarter will amount to approximately £35, so he enters this figure in the space for the appropriate month and adjusts his additions. The sheet should now look like Table 3.4 (page 39).

When the bank balance lines have been filled in, the cash flow forecast is complete, and Alexander notes with pleasure that he stands a good chance of having over £400 in the bank by the end of June. This is, of course, not his profit for the six months; on the one hand, he has drawn out £3,000, and on the other, he still owes – to his suppliers and Doreen Gray, among others – over £150.

Although he is determined never to be overdrawn by more than £250 if he can help it, Alexander has shown prudence in asking for an overdraft facility of £500. This amount should cover him against the unexpected crises that can occur in business when least expected.

In Chapter 12 you will see how Battersby & Co got on and how Alexander used this forecast as a simple budgetary control.

For a very long time the small shopkeeper was like the independent tradesperson, such as Alexander Battersby, the typical very small entrepreneur. Running a little shop was a natural way of life to many people. It had many advantages. Very often one 'lived above the shop' which could lead to a close family life; it appealed to those who liked their fellow men and women and gave great scope for meeting and talking with them, and unlike Alexander Battersby's profession it needed, many thought, very little training. It was simply a matter of choosing a satisfactory site, with many feet passing the door, and a careful control over stock and a pleasant life could ensue. But it all depended on the lifestyle of the customers. In the past most women married and became housewives. To them the daily shopping was almost a social occasion. It got you out of the house and you met friends and acquaintances. But such a way of life has largely gone. The high overheads, relative to turnover, in a shop that dealt with customers on an individual basis, one by one, became prohibitive except for expensive items.

Let us see what happened in the closing days of the 'corner' shop, as this illustrates the inherent problems of the small retailer.

Example 3.2: Nicola Grant

Nicola Grant had been in touch with an agency listing small shops and businesses for sale, and became interested in a grocery business about which she had been sent details. The asking price of the business, including the lock-up property, was £42,500 'plus stock at valuation'. On further enquiry, she learnt that the property itself was valued at £32,000, leaving £10,500 for goodwill and fixtures (not including the bacon slicer and fridge which, Nicola found later, were on hire purchase). The estimated value of the stock was £16,000.

Nicola had been given a copy of a trading and profit and loss account for the year ending July 2002. It had been explained that the accountants, Messrs Edward Gibbon & Co, had not yet completed those for 2002–03. The accounts for 2002 had the figures for 2001 alongside and looked like Table 3.5.

Nicola was impressed by the increasing profit, which the vendors (the Smiths) told her was because of 'better buying'. When she said she could not afford to buy the property, they offered to let it to her on a lease for £3,000 a year, 'tenant to pay all repairs, with an option to buy at a price to be agreed'.

Although £3,000 would be cut off the net profit, Nicola felt that £4,237 a year – or £80 a week – was still worth having, and she had always, since childhood, wanted to run a little shop. Some friends at a party told her that if she were to add more lines, such as wines and spirits, they would all buy from her, and the shop could be a 'little gold mine'.

She approached the bank and was given a sympathetic hearing, but was advised to go to the Ourtown Enterprise Agency for guidance in the drawing up of a cash flow forecast and business plan. Nicola explained to the counsellor at the agency that she had £4,000 saved up with a building society and that her father would lend her £9,000 more to set her up in business. As the goodwill, stock and fixtures would come to £26,500, she would have to borrow £13,500 from the bank, offering her home as security.

When the counsellor examined the accounts, his face took on a rather solemn expression. He suggested to Nicola that they draw up a list of what the overheads were likely to be the following year, with Nicola running the shop. Together they produced a chart (see Table 3.6).

The counsellor pointed out that this level of overheads would leave Nicola with only £2,226 profit to live on – less than £43 per

Table 3.5   Mr & Mrs Smith (Quality Food Shop)

Trading Account
Year ended 31 July 2002

	2002		2001	
	£	£	£	£
Sales		76,076		78,542
Stock at start	13,673		12,524	
Purchases	61,752		65,283	
	75,425		77,807	
Stock at end	15,780		13,630	
		59,645		64,177
Gross profit		£16,431		£14,365

Profit and loss account
Year ended 31 July 2002

		2002	2001	
Gross profit		16,431	14,365	
less wages and NIC	3,934		3,927	
Rates and insurance	792		750	
Heat and light	775		690	
Telephone	275		272	
Bags and wrapping	179		185	
Motor expenses	2,116		1,935	
Repairs	311		270	
Sundries	217		193	
Bank charges	45		50	
Accountancy	450		400	
Hire purchase	100		50	
		9,914	8,722	
Profit for the year		£7,237	£5,643	

Table 3.6 Nicola Grant's list of overheads

	£	
Wages	3,500	Nicola would still need part-time help
Rent	3,000	
Rates and insurance	825	
Heat and light	780	
Telephone	150	Nicola would be economical
Bags and wrapping	150	
Accountancy	450	
Repairs	350	Nicola agreed much needed to be done
Motor expenses	2,500	Nicola would still have to go to the cash and carry wholesalers
Sundries	225	
Hire purchase	250	The fridge had been acquired since the last account
Interest	2,025	£13,500 at 15%
Total	£14,205	

week – out of a gross profit as shown for 2002 (£16,431). Moreover, as the counsellor said, the turnover seemed to be going down rather than up, and it was doubtful whether in 2004 the 2002 sales could be maintained.

Nicola was horrified by these figures, and for a moment or two at least, she hated the counsellor for spoiling her lovely dream. There was no argument, however. Unless the turnover were to increase dramatically, there would be no real profit from the business. Nicola knew her party friends too well to believe that they would go out of their way to bring trade to her shop, and even if they did, their purchases would amount to no more than a pittance. The counsellor pointed out that to stock up with wines would cost money and there was no guarantee of sales. In his opinion the business was hardly worth buying, and certainly 'goodwill' should not figure as an item in the price.

Nicola decided to make one further effort, however. She went back to see the Smiths and told them what the counsellor had said. They were outraged. They then 'confessed' to Nicola that they had taken

£75 a week 'at least' out of the business before declaring their income for tax.

Nicola returned to give the counsellor this additional information, but he had 'heard that one before'. While it could have been just possible in 2001, when an extra £75 a week added to the turnover would have produced a gross profit of 22 per cent, such an addition to the 2002 figures would have produced a gross profit of 25.4 per cent, far beyond the average for a shop of that type.

Nicola took the point and, sighing, decided to abandon the project.

Opening a small shop such as a gift shop can seem an attractive option and it might indeed prosper in a holiday resort. However, such a venture needs thorough investigation, as there is always the danger that it will be less successful on cold October days in workaday streets when mortgages are pressing.

4

Retail and catering

Britain is a nation of traders. Our financial system is in many ways geared for trading rather than for making goods. The 'money people' understand and sympathize with trading projects much more readily than with schemes for manufacturing.

This in itself harbours dangers for the person who wishes to open or buy a retail business. Britain is full of brilliant, aggressive traders: wholesale traders, traders in goods, traders in stocks and bonds. Whatever the commodity, there is a Smith, a Jones, a MacTavish, a Shah or a Patel busily trading in it, making use of all his or her skill and experience, and backed by a supportive financial system. The competition is terrific. It starts at the top. The enterprise and cut-throat ruthlessness of the great corporations filter down, affecting the small side-street shops and making the earning of a decent living very hard indeed.

Nevertheless, as a retailer you will probably get a relatively sympathetic hearing from the banker, who has not only an inherent understanding of the trade, but also two other reasons for his or her preference. The first is psychological. When a manufacturer goes bust, it does so pretty dramatically, and egg gets splashed on many faces. The failure of a shop is a much slower process as a rule – a steady descent into poverty and squalor. It goes almost unnoticed except by the victims. The second reason for a banker's preference is based on the fact that it is often possible to sell even a moribund retail shop. If one person fails, another will be along, convinced of making a go of it. The British yearn to be shopkeepers and often possess not only a touching faith in their ability to run such a business, but quite often the cash as well, by way of redundancy money, to buy one, however derelict.

Be that as it may, the retailer presenting a business plan retains an inbuilt advantage in that the banker does know what is being talked about. It is highly unlikely that the banker is also a scientist or an engineer or has spent time in a factory, but he or she will have been in a shop and will know what goes on there. So the retailer will have far less explaining to do. There will be no need to translate a lot of technical jargon. Furthermore, if he or she has been living in the area for more than a few months, the banker will almost certainly know the location of the shop in question and the pattern of trade. This should also cut down on the need for words.

'So why,' you will ask, 'should I write an elaborate business plan? Why not just send in the required cash flow forecast, copies of accounts supplied by the vendor and a covering letter?'

First, despite the understanding and sympathy many bankers feel for traders as against manufacturers, they do know that many retail shops lose money. Experience has shown that even if the bank recovers its money, there is often very little left for the owner. Your banker is not an ogre. He or she will want to be assured that you are not making a bad mistake and fully understand what it is you are proposing to undertake.

Second, the principle laid down in Chapter 1 applies with at least equal force to retail business. Writing a comprehensive business plan is the best way of ensuring that the strategy and tactics to be employed are well thought-out and logical. There are more dangers and difficulties entailed in running a retail business than most people think.

Two questions require particular attention: what is the market for your goods, and what should your buying policy be?

The market

- Is there a sufficient market for your goods in the catchment area of your shop?
- What must your share of the market be to enable you to make a reasonable profit?
  - How many pairs of feet will be passing your shop each day?
  - How many of these will turn into the shop, ie become customers?
  - How much will each customer have to spend to give you a reasonable annual profit?
  - Are the 'multiples' getting an increasing share of the trade in your goods?

Questions like this must be asked and the answers entered in your business plan.

Your buying policy

If you have chosen the right site and the right type of goods to sell, the surest way of losing money is through bad buying. You must work out a sensible buying policy based on your expected monthly rate of sales and the ratio of stock to cost of goods sold. Set down that policy in your business plan. If you are going to employ an organized system of stock control – and you ought to do so – say so, and give an outline of your methods. How often will you do a physical stocktake? The more frequently you do one, the greater will be your stock control over your business.

There are, of course, other problems that a retailer may face, to do with employment of staff or security of tenure, for instance, but the two that are common to all retailing are choice of site and buying of stock. These are the two aspects of the business about which you must write a great deal in your business plan, no matter what type of retail operation yours is.

'The English' sneered Napoleon Bonaparte, 'are a nation of shopkeepers'. It would have been far better for the world if the young Corsican had himself kept a shop in his native country rather than plunging all Europe into long wars in his search for power and glory.

But Britain is a nation of traders, and our financial system is in many ways more sympathetic to those trading than to those making goods. In an era in which cash flow is of supreme importance, retailers have one very big advantage. Usually they sell for cash and buy on credit. The more they trade, the faster the cash rolls in. This allows the successful shopkeeper to expand almost without limit, unlike manufacturers whose success usually brings problems of finance. The latter have to pay out more and more for wages and materials while waiting to be paid by their expanding list of customers. A century ago successful retail expansion involved setting up branches in other towns. Mr Boot of Nottingham successfully spread his shops over the whole of the United Kingdom as a result of his fine positive cash flow.

Mr Boot's shops are still there, largely thanks to the dispensing service they offer, but not, say, Mr Lipton's grocery stores, which once were a feature of every High Street. It was possible until recently for an independent shopkeeper, if clever and popular with his or her customers, to compete with the 'multiples'. But it is the supermarkets that now are almost completely dominant, crushing independent and multiple alike. We must admit that they do this deservedly, offering services in tune with life as it is lived in the 21st century. They have markedly reduced the cost of household shopping to all by cutting out so many of the counter hands who had to wait on the individual customer, and they have made it possible for bachelors and women with jobs to shop once a fortnight, and take all their normal shopping away in one trolley. Not only has life speeded up, the shopping basket of groceries is a far smaller proportion of most family budgets.

Moreover the history of small business since *How to Prepare a Business Plan* was first written has been one of increasingly burdensome regulations. Now the cost of complying with a regulation, however plausible it may sound, always falls far, far harder as a percentage of turnover on a small enterprise than on the big PLC with its own voice in the CBI.

In many cases a small enterprise has been crushed by the sheer cost of doing what the bureaucrats demand, and far more have been discouraged from going in for expansion. In the days when lawyers knew Latin there was a humane maxim, full of common sense, which said *De minimis non curat lex* (trifles are not the concern of the law). But, increasingly, the law does concern itself with trifles, such as prosecuting elderly ladies for selling sweets by the ounce rather than by the gram. Small businesses are easier meat than powerful public companies.

Technology has, as so often, come to the aid of the underprivileged, this time in the shape of the internet which is, for all its faults, a splendid challenge by the entrepreneurial spirit to the deadening hand of over-regulation. There are two main ways for a trader to use the internet. One, which I think of as the clever amateur's way, is to use eBay. The other, more seriously professional, is to set up your own website. Each has its own advantages.

The eBay system is a modern method of carrying out something akin to an old-fashioned auction. It has many advantages:

- You do not need special premises, only a computer and a connection with the internet.
- Anyone within the limits of the polar ice, north or south, can use it, either for buying or selling, and even at the poles themselves if you can arrange delivery of the goods.
- To the computer-aware it is simple: just log on and follow the instructions given.
- There is a system whereby the public and especially the eBay users can gain knowledge of the standing of any other user. Sellers and buyers are both required to record their satisfaction or dissatisfaction with the transaction, adding comments. As all this is recorded for all parties it is easy to see how a good, or bad, reputation can very quickly be built up, and honesty becomes the necessary policy.

This reputation is of great value. Vendors, and purchasers, both cherish their good reputations and defend them vigorously. Many who have their own website still use eBay and advertise their good record thereon so as to maintain and enhance their reputation. It is also used by vendors with their own shops to widen their range of customers, especially for those with unusual goods to offer.

But there are weaknesses in relying on eBay. Some may wish to save the percentage that is charged on the transactions. Others may find the auction element a deterrent and would prefer a fixed price system. Another important feature is time. From the time you decide to sell something on eBay to the time you have completed all the negotiations with the buyer and have got your money, a deal of time will have elapsed. In a paragraph above I emphasized the importance to a retailer of cash flow. Any delay in getting your money loses that retailers' advantage. Having your own website can reduce any time delay.

Your website is your very own 'shop'. On it you can exhibit anything you choose (except libels, excitements to racism and child pornography). You can list the goods and services you are offering and praise them to the full, as long as you do not mislead the customer, and you can publish genuine testimonials. You will publish your terms of sale and delivery, the methods of payment you will accept and the way you want any payment to be guaranteed. You will, of course, be very unwilling, to say the least, to dispatch goods before payment. The trust must be both ways, and here, if you have been trading on eBay, you will have the advantage of a fine eBay record, which you can advertise. Some internet traders use both methods, using their good record on eBay to increase the repute on the website.

Let us see how a young person set out to sell on the internet.

Example 4.1: Flurry Knox

One of Flurry's real names was Florence; his parents had called him so in the hope that his very rich great-aunt would leave him a fortune. She didn't. Flurry had to earn his own living. He had been familiar with computers from an early age. He had not, however, gone so far as some of his friends as to lose virtually all interest in the terrestrial world, or in his native language, and be only capable of communicating in computerese and a series of grunts. Moreover, as a schoolboy he had been a great collector of things: postage stamps, curios and all. He became adept at trading such things with his friends and acquaintances. Later, he found visits to car boot sales and the like to be rewarding. He even used eBay on the internet. Bored with his jobs after leaving school, he decided to venture on internet selling as a way of earning a good living.

His decision was confirmed when he reflected that on the internet his market would not be limited to those who could come to his shop or even to the inhabitants of the United Kingdom. The whole world could come to his website! He would launch his trading argosy into the vastness of 'cyberspace'. Here there would be a market for the rarest and most unusual goods. What is more, so long as he obeys the common law, pays his proper taxes and treats his customers fairly, he is free from petty regulations. It looked like a doddle.

There is one feature of trading that is worth keeping in mind, even on the internet. I call this the 'minimum profitable sale' problem. Many years ago I worked out for a shopkeeping client that, with his overheads and staff costs, to make a sale per customer of less than 8/6d (42.5p) was to trade at a real loss, even when the mark-up was a generous one. This accounts for the disappearance of those very useful little shops that would sell you a reel of cotton, a packet of needles or a few screws when you wanted them, and for the disappearance into filling stations of those small tobacco and sweetie shops that used to exist in every street. With the general increase in wages, rent, rates, taxes and so on, the minimum profitable sale in a shop has shown an astronomical increase. You will have noticed that supermarkets always close down the quick-service (no more than 10 items per basket) outlets first, and concentrate on the shoppers with full trolleys where the total transaction will be a hefty one. You will have noticed that the remaining small shops in the high street all sell expensive items – 'designer' clothes, jewellery and the like.

Flurry had been for years an enthusiastic restorer of classic motorbikes. An old Norton or a Scott machine would send him into raptures, but they were very few and far between and spares were incredibly difficult to obtain either as originals or as replicas. Flurry was used to using eBay to trawl for rare items, and used his once hated nickname, Flurry, as his identifier.

Although Flurry had added to his bank account very nicely through his amateur dealings on eBay, he realized that he was now in a different situation. He would need additional capital, which he hoped would come from a bank, and he would have to formalize his working procedures as a guide book for his journey into the new world, as recommended in the introduction to this book.

Although he was prepared to sell any unconsidered trifle on eBay, he decided to concentrate on trading motorbikes, and his proposal to potential financial backers was as follows:

"My name is Florence McCarthy Knox and I live at 27 Blackstone Road, Witherspool. I have been making a substantial profit on deals on the internet using the system called eBay. I now propose to give up my regular job, which I am finding uninteresting, and devote my whole working time to trading on the internet with my own website. I shall need working capital of £20,000 of which I can supply £7,500 of my own."

The market

Although the market for unusual motorbikes, spare parts and memorabilia in any one country is somewhat limited, the internet will give me access to anywhere in the world in which there are roads for bikes to travel on. Spare parts are often hard to come by and enthusiasts have a growing demand for the memorabilia of the sport – old entrance tickets, copies of old manuals, magazines and the like. I myself have been able to sell on eBay documents regarding the once famous rider Stanley Woods in the 1920s, and for a very good price. In the past year I have been able to sell on eBay over £10,000 worth of goods, and with a personal website and with advertising in Europe-wide motorbike magazines and working full time I expect to increase that business several-fold.

About myself

I am not married. I live with my widowed mother. I rent an old warehouse where I keep any stock and where my friend Peter Spratt and I spend our time at weekends restoring classic bikes. We have done well at this, selling our machines on eBay. Whether we will combine this activity with my trading venture, I do not know. Peter has not made up his mind.

What I shall do right away

The first thing to do is to set up my website. Although I am an experienced internet user I shall take the advice of a specialist in this matter. My present computer is several years old so it is time I bought a more powerful one. I shall need office equipment as I must keep hard copy of much of my correspondence, and some kind of stock control system, as in many cases I will buy in bulk and sell retail. My existing warehouse will be adequate, at least for the time being. Dispatch will, I hope, become a problem and I shall have to arrange for stores of packing and wrapping materials.

Already I have made contact with publishers of cycle magazines both here and on the continent, ready for the time I launch my project.

There are, throughout the world, manufacturers of motorbikes with only small sales in the United Kingdom and in parts of Europe generally. I am in touch with such people with regard to setting up agencies for their spares, and also if possible for their machines, as well as trading in spare parts for obsolete bikes, of which I shall try to build up a stock both of spare parts and in the 'memorabilia' department.

The money I shall need

Initially, I calculate, I shall need £7,000 for initial expenses as indicated above, to provide me with money to live on when I have given up my job, and for buying my initial stock. If all goes to plan my working capital will have to increase, possibly up to £20,000. This is best covered by an overdraft facility. I have £3,000 in the bank, which will go into the new business account; and my mother has agreed to guarantee the overdraft with her house, free of mortgage. She has further securities, if necessary, to support me.

I intend to put as much of my profits as possible back into the business to build up my working capital.

In the introduction, the importance of having an 'edge' over the competition was emphasized. Unfortunately, finding an edge is often more difficult for the would-be shop owner than it is for the small manufacturer or someone in a service trade.

The large chain stores are so powerful in controlling the distribution of well-advertised lines that it is impossible to compete with them on price. Competing on 'service', in the old sense of giving personal attention to customers, is of little real value except in the case of technical goods. Retail service these days means, for the most part, providing a large supermarket where a family with a working mother can do all the regular shopping for a fortnight under one roof and take it all away in one trolley. Nor is having a little local monopoly on a fringe housing estate much good. More and more families have cars and do their shopping in a shopping centre. The crumbs that fall from the big high-street stores are rarely able to support the small local shops nowadays.

What remains for the small retail trader? Well, special knowledge and skill, for a start. The classic example is the dispensing chemist, where trade is still to a great extent in private hands. But to become a qualified dispensing chemist requires years of training. Selling high-class jewellery, specialized photographic equipment and the like successfully also requires a high degree of knowledge. And a considerable investment of both time and money is needed to establish a reputation and to acquire a sufficiently wide stockholding.

If there is a little 'making' as well as 'selling' in your shops, this can provide the necessary edge. Bakers bake as well as sell their bread and cakes. Butchers cut up their meat as well as hand it out over the counter. To make and sell is often a better bet, if the market is there and your product is really superior, than just to resell other firms' merchandise.

Sometimes it is possible to find a 'niche'. There may be a demand for some class of goods not being supplied by the high-street shops. If you are sure that the market is big enough and that you can capture it, this is almost certainly the best edge you can get. But you will need to do a great deal of market research and remain ever vigilant to ensure that you remain ahead of anyone who attempts to compete.

In my next example the entrepreneur is banking on:

- know-how concerning a special range of goods;
- having found a niche in the market;
- an ingenious idea for helping to keep some major customers 'loyal'.

Example 4.2: Robert Herrick and Deirdre Williams

Ourtown Electrical Supplies Ltd is acquiring the shop hitherto run by Joe Lamplight in Dogberry Street, Ourtown. Additional capital of £40,000 is needed to extend the services it offers to the electrical contractors in the borough.

History of the existing business

Joe Lamplight's father opened a shop selling electrical goods in High Street, Ourtown in 1960. He retired in 1996, when the High Street property was acquired by Pachyderm Developments plc under a compulsory purchase order of the then Ourtown Metropolitan Borough Council.

In order to carry on the business, Joe Lamplight took a lease on premises in Dogberry Street. This lease is about to expire and Joe, having reached retirement age, has offered the goodwill and stock of the business for sale.

The trade in large items of electrical household equipment such as cookers and TV sets has declined over the years, but the shop has maintained a steady turnover in the smaller items, especially lamps and light fittings. Sales to the public account for about half the turnover, sales at trade discount terms to local electricians and electrical contractors for the remainder.

In 2006 the turnover amounted to £79,000 and the gross profit to £19,250. The current stock is valued at £17,000, and Mr Lamplight is asking an additional £4,000 in consideration of his existing connections.

It is not intended to renew the lease at Dogberry Street. The company has obtained an option on the ground floor of the Ourtown Co-operative Society's former emporium in Verges Street. Although this is some distance from the main shopping centre, it is deemed suitable for the purposes of the company. A lease for 20 years is available at an initial annual rent of £10,250.

The market

Our initial marketing thrust will be directed to supplying the electrical contractors in Ourtown and surrounding districts. We shall maintain the existing retail trade and, indeed, increase our range.

Our long-term policy will be to establish a comprehensive retail trade in both electrical and electronic goods.

There are 29 electrical contractors in Ourtown and 20 more in the catchment area, which includes Witherspool. The value of goods bought by those individuals and firms we have canvassed greatly exceeds £500,000 a year. Many of these purchases will be made directly from the manufacturers, but at least two-thirds are obtained through wholesale suppliers in Bradfield, 20 miles distant over congested roads.

Lamplights have been attempting to meet this demand and are well thought of, but shortage of both money for stock and space to store and display has limited the opportunities.

A canvas has been made of 30 of the potential customers, and this has produced a very encouraging response. There have been complaints, sometimes very bitter, about the infrequency and unreliability of the Bradfield suppliers' out-of-town deliveries, and a local supplier with a comprehensive stock would be very welcome.

Ten of the contractors have gone so far as to agree to invest in the new company, and Messrs Belt & Braces, Chartered Accountants, have suggested that use could be made of Enterprise Investment Scheme rules, enabling investment to be made by these contractors out of taxable income. This has been approved by the investors' own accountants.

The directors

There are three directors of Ourtown Electrical Supplies Ltd.

Robert Herrick will be managing director, with direct responsibility for both trade sales and running the shop. He has been, for the past five years, the manager of the Bradfield branch of Electron Suppliers Ltd, running almost exactly the same type of business. He had increased the turnover and profit for Electron every year by a greater margin than was shown by any other branch, but left because he saw no possibility for further promotion. Robert is married with one child. He has a BSc from London University and has attended management courses at Bradfield University's Department of Business Studies.

Joseph Lamplight, the present proprietor of the business, has agreed to stay on as a part-time director for at least one year. He will attend the business as and when required. His experience of Ourtown conditions – he is a Rotarian and a member of the Chamber of Commerce – will be extremely valuable, as will his friendly relations with many of the customers. He will give all the help he can in the setting up of the new organization.

Deirdre Williams, a graduate of Bradfield University, was, before her marriage, secretary to the regional chairman of the Home Counties Bank. Three years ago she returned to commerce as personal assistant to a director of Pachyderm Developments plc. She finds, however, that opportunities in this job are limited and has joined Robert Herrick to run this company. She will be in charge of administration and all financial aspects of the company.

Robert Herrick will provide £20,000 capital; Deirdre Williams £10,000. Each will receive a salary of £12,000 per annum. Joseph Lamplight will receive £2,000 a year for his services and advice, payable quarterly.

Accountants are Messrs Belt & Braces.

Solicitors are Messrs Reed, Herring and Co of Dover Court, Ourtown.

Methods

On 30 November it is intended to move the whole of the existing stock to the new premises. These will have been refitted as a show-room, where members of the public as well as the trade purchasers can examine and select from the stock. There are extensive stock-rooms at the rear and limited parking facilities by a side entrance where trade customers can pick up goods. The company's suppliers and own van driver can also use this entrance.

The company will offer the trade customers 25 per cent off list price, with additional discounts of 2.5 per cent for payment within 30 days and 7.5 per cent for cash on delivery. Delivery will be free within 10 miles for orders of more than £100, but a charge of £5 will be made for smaller orders. The company intends to make deliveries within eight hours inside this 10-mile radius.

The managing director plans to visit all trade clients and potential trade clients at least once every two months.

A brochure and a price list of the company's main lines and items have been designed and are being printed.

On 7 December the company intends to open at the new premises with a formal gala to which all potential trade customers will be invited, together with the local press. Bobby Lovebird, the actress, who is, of course, a local girl, has kindly consented to be present for the formal opening ceremony.

One of the company's major concerns will be the proper control of purchasing and stock levels, and with this aim in view, it has engaged the services of Hepplewhite and Co to design a computerized stock control system. The directors believe that at £15,000 this system should pay for itself within a very short period.

Longer-term strategy

The directors have mapped out a five-year plan. In the earlier phases, the company will concentrate on the type of trade outlined above. However, sales to the public will not be neglected, and when the time is ripe, both financially and as indicated by a market survey, a major project for the sale of larger electrical items, such as cookers, washing machines, etc will be launched. This will probably necessitate raising more capital.

In five years EIS investors in the company will be in a position to receive the rewards of their investment. It is hoped they will continue as shareholders, but in any case the company expects to be able to offer reasonable terms to buy them out, probably by means of a new share issue.

This is a company looking to expand, not only in the short term, but also to become a major trading organization.

Financial requirements

The capital already subscribed or agreed to be subscribed is shown in Table 4.1.

Table 4.1   Money subscribed for the business

	£	
Robert Herrick	20,000	
Deirdre Williams	10,000	
Joseph Lamplight	4,000	(in satisfaction of the goodwill of his business)
Trade (EIS) subscribers	20,000	
Total	£54,000	

The directors are asking for a development loan of £30,000 and an overdraft facility, to take care of temporary cash shortfalls, of £10,000

The initial expenditure will be as shown in Table 4.2.

The balance of £6,500, together with the overdraft facility, should provide sufficient working capital, as will be seen from the enclosed cash flow forecast.

Table 4.2 Initial expenditure of the business

	£
Payment to Joe Lamplight for stock	17,000
Additional starting stock	12,000
Fittings and alterations to new premises and van	12,500
Computer and software	20,000
Advertising and publicity	5,000
Six months' rent in advance	5,000
Sundries	2,000
Total	£73,500

Financial forecasts

On the basis of forecasts of sales and costs, Messrs Belt & Braces have produced the enclosed statements of anticipated overheads, profits and cash flow.

As will be seen in Table 4.3, the directors are budgeting for a profit of £9,000, a bank balance of £14,000, and reduction of the term loan by repayment of £18,000. If the budgeted figures are fulfilled, the balance sheets at the end of the year should look like Table 4.4.

The directors do not propose to pay a dividend for at least the first year but will use the anticipated cash surplus to develop the retail side of the business, ie the sale of refrigerators, cookers, TV sets, etc.

In the second year, if all goes well, it is hoped to achieve a turnover of £500,000, with a net profit of £35,000.

Table 4.3 Ourtown financial projections for first year of trading

Ourtown Electrical Supplies Ltd

Financial projections for first year of trading

Overhead schedule	Month 12	Month 1	Month 2	Month 3	Month 4	Month 5	Month 6	Month 7	Month 8	Month 9	Month 10	Month 11	Carry forward	Total
Rent	5,126						2,563			2,563				10,252
Rates	305	305	305	305	305	305	305	305	305	305				3,050
Directors' fees	1,667	1,667	2,166	1,667	1,667	2,166	1,667	1,667	2,166	1,667	1,667	2,166		22,000
Electricity				700			600			550			700	2,550
Gas				200			150			100			175	625
Insurance (inc motor)	875													875
Bank charges			75			75			75			75		300
Licence fees (inc motor)	100													100
Wages	1,800	1,800	1,800	1,800	1,800	1,800	1,800	1,800	1,800	1,800	1,800	1,800		21,600
PAYE and NICs				378			378			378			378	1,512
Total non-VATable	9,873	3,772	4,346	5,050	3,772	4,346	7,463	3,772	4,346	7,363	3,467	4,041	1,253	62,864
Advertising	5,000	150	150	150	150	150	150	150	150	150	150	150		6,650
Petrol and oil	120	120	120	120	120	120	120	120	120	120	120	120		1,440
Motor repairs			100			100			100			100		400
Telephone	200			175			175			175			175	900
Sundries	100	100	100	100	100	100	100	100	100	100	100	100		1,200
Professional fees	750			200			200			200			400	1,750
Total VATable	6,170	370	470	745	370	470	745	370	470	745	370	470	575	12,340
VAT	1,080	65	82	130	65	82	130	65	82	130	65	82		2,158
Total overheads	17,123	4,207	4,898	5,925	4,207	4,898	8,338	4,207	4,898	8,238	3,902	4,593		75,204

Table 4.3 *continued*

Profit and loss account

	Month 12	Month 1	Month 2	Month 3	Month 4	Month 5	Month 6	Month 7	Month 8	Month 9	Month 10	Month 11	Total
Sales	27,500	21,500	23,250	26,600	29,600	29,600	29,600	29,600	22,200	34,000	37,000	37,000	347,450
less													
Cost of goods sold	18,163	15,865	16,838	19,355	21,680	21,680	21,680	21,680	16,260	24,775	27,100	27,100	252,176
Overheads	6,267	6,267	6,267	6,267	6,267	6,267	6,267	6,267	6,267	6,267	6,267	6,267	75,204
Interest on overdraft			70	68									138
Interest on loan	333	315	298	280	263	245	228	210	193	175	158	140	2,838
Depreciation	677	677	677	677	677	677	677	677	677	677	677	677	8,124
Net profit	2060	–1,624	–900	–47	713	731	748	766	–1,197	2,106	2,798	2,816	8,970

Note: At the time Mr Herrick had this forecast drawn up there was no VAT on fuel

Table 4.4   Projected balance sheets for the business

Fixed Assets	£	£
Goodwill		4,000
Fittings and equipment	32,500	
less Depreciation	8,125	
		24,375
		28,375
Current Assets		
Stock	29,000	
Debtors	35,145	
Cash	14,880	
	79,025	
Current Liabilities		
Creditors	26,218	
VAT	6,212	
	32,430	
Net Current Assets		46,595
		74,970
Long-term loan	30,000	
less repayments	18,000	
		12,000
		62,970
Capital and Reserves		
Share capital		54,000
Profit and loss account		8,970
Shareholders' funds		62,970

Catering

One of the most flourishing of small-scale enterprises over the past few years has been the opening of restaurants, and the catering business in general has flourished. Increasing prosperity over the past 20 years and a greater sense of adventure in food and wine have turned the simple 'cut-off-the-joint-and-two-veg' feeding of travellers into a major industry, an industry that still remains substantially in the hands of the small entrepreneur. So a few comments on business planning for small eating places seem called for.

Anyone who has been a small business adviser will know people who say that their business or profession is so special that they need no advice except on such points as how to charm (or con) money out of a bank. But the general principles of planning, and running, a successful business apply even to the most special of activities.

Chapter 1 mentioned a writer who claimed that if you invented a better mousetrap, all the world would beat a path to your door. There never was a statement more false, and the comment voices an assumption that has led many people with a good idea into disaster. You may be the best cook and the best designer of tasty meals within 50 miles, but that will not automatically draw customers to you. And if you cannot get customers to come into your restaurant and cannot make the meals yield you a profit, you will be no more successful than someone who can only just about boil an egg.

Let us start with the basics. First, what kind of restaurant do you want to run? An up-market place for the local gourmets; or something to appeal to the 'cut-off-the-joint' people mentioned above? Perhaps something more cheap and cheerful, competing in the fast-food market or running something like a lorry-drivers' pull-in, or even a sandwich bar, would give you more satisfaction.

As regards the sandwich bar, and, indeed, all forms of take-away outlet, these are more related to retailing than to catering. As stated earlier in this chapter, making as well as selling helps a small retailer to survive in these days of fierce competition by national and international companies. The problems, then, of the take-away are those of the retail shop, namely the selection of premises as handy as possible for your customers and at a reasonable rent. With a good site at a fair price, if you maintain a good standard of product and keep on the right side of all bureaucrats and tax officials, you should do reasonably well.

The would-be supplier of what I have called the 'cut-off-the-joint' catering is caught between a rock and a hard place. On the one hand, it is the type of cooking that a family gets at home, and on the other it is the first, and usually only, choice for the tenants of licensed premises who want to add 'pub grub' to help pay the rent. These tenants start with the advantages of greatly reduced overheads and a site with an already existing clientele. A formidable competition is set up between eating out with them and cooking at home.

This section is therefore written with special reference to those restaurateurs who are trying to sell either specialist or the very best of European cuisine. Such a one is Osbert Wilkinson.

Example 4.3: Osbert Wilkinson

Osbert Wilkinson has much experience in the catering trade and has persuaded his friend, Guy Loosley, a brilliant chef, to join him in starting a classy restaurant in a provincial town. Osbert decides that his most likely customers will be as follows. First, the couples, or foursomes, who are out to make an 'occasion' out of the meal. Second, the business person who wants to impress a colleague or a potential customer with his of her savoir-faire and taste. And finally, the retired couple for whom cooking is now nothing but a chore and who have developed individual tastes and are not satisfied with fast food or 'pub grub'.

Having made the strategic decision to cater for these – shall we say, sophisticated – customers, he will plan his marketing and make his design decisions accordingly. His leaflets, advertisements in the local press, and the menus he will hang beside the door will be targeted at such customers. Moreover, the design and décor of the place must be such that the sense of occasion is maintained. The atmosphere of the place must be inviting and such as to make, say, the romantic couple want to come again and again. Everyone knows of restaurants that look as if an old British Rail waiting room has been fitted out with tables and chairs from a long defunct Co-op. The cooking has to be absolutely superb, with the most imaginative dishes, to overcome such a handicap.

Osbert knows he has the tremendous gift of remembering faces and the ability to put names to them. Seeing a guest come in and being able, right away, to say 'Nice to see you again, Mr Blackwell' starts the evening well, and puts the customer already in a good mood. This talent of Osbert's is of supreme value to a restaurateur. A smile costs nothing, and he will train his waiting staff to keep their good-looking faces smiling a welcome however much pressure they are under. He will also emphasize to all his staff that hospitality begins from the moment the telephone is picked up when anyone calls to make a booking. Charm and efficiency in this area is an essential feature of success. It continues all the time the customer is on the premises, in that all staff from the major-domo, if there is one, to the most junior waiter should never let any client feel that he or she is being neglected. The staff should keep their eyes wandering around the room to see whether any customers look as if they need something.

The slogan in the property world is 'Location, location, location'. The slogan in the world of catering should be 'Overheads, overheads, overheads'. A caterer's overheads are huge compared with the costs of the food and drink he or she supplies and the day-to-day sundries' costs. Failure to anticipate what overheads he or she will incur, especially as regards staff costs and failure to control them rigidly, are the cause of many failures.

Osbert's accountant adviser tells him to produce a break-even analysis, as outlined in Chapter 2. Osbert must make sure that his gross profit on the food and wine will more than cover the costs he will incur before he even puts on the oven for his first client's meal.

It has already been decided that Osbert will open a medium-sized restaurant, of say 50 places, in premises at a rent of £15,000 per year. Osbert estimates that, even if he only opens for dinners, he will need staff (excluding himself) of three (including his friend Guy) in the kitchen and three waiters or waitresses. These should cover the work for most evenings, with part-timers on Saturday and, he hopes, Fridays and Sundays too. He will have to borrow extensively to set it all up and there will be interest to pay. Market research indicates that he can charge £25 per head in the evening, including a bottle of wine at £15 per pair of diners.

He and the accountant together work out the overheads forecast shown in Table 4.5.

If Osbert opens six days a week for 52 weeks, this means that his overheads will cost him £369 (£115,000 ÷ 312) per day. He expects to get £25 per person per evening (£17.50 for food, £7.50 for wine) which is £21.50 (approximately) net of VAT. The marginal cost of this is (again net of VAT):

Food	£4.375
Wine	£3.325
Sundries	£0.300
Total	£8.000

Table 4.5   Overheads forecast for Osbert Wilkinson's restaurant

A. Standing overheads	£	£
Rent	15,000	
Rates	5,000	
Interest on loans	8,000	
Own minimal living costs	10,000	38,000
B. Variable overheads		
Staff	60,000	
Heating, light, etc	8,000	
Insurance and accountancy	2,000	
Miscellaneous	7,000	77,000
	Total	£115,000

Therefore, his gross profit per person per evening (£21.25 – £8) is £13.25.

From this the accountant calculates that Osbert must have an average of 28 (369/13.25) persons per night just to cover his inevitable overheads and his own minimal living costs. This last must be calculated in; if the proprietor of the enterprise can't continue to exist, the project will fail anyway.

The accountant also calculated how many extra customers would be required per evening to turn the minimum amount allocated to Osbert's own living costs into a profit of £20,000. It will be £10,000 ÷ 13.25 ÷ 312 = 2.4. (Such a calculation emphasizes the importance not only of controlling overheads but of showing how, once you have once crossed the profit-making line, your rewards will climb steeply (until you find you need an extra staff member). Later I hope to give some hints as to how this progress can be maintained.

The next question raised was whether the restaurant should open for lunches so as to use the gross profit from them to help with the overheads. Osbert pointed out that the lunch trade was rather different from that of the evening. At night people go out for an hour or so's enjoyment. It is an alternative, or supplement to, the cinema or to the theatre, not just a way of staving off hunger. Lunch customers are not always different, of course; there are often meetings of old friends or business associates for lunch, but generally it is a low-key affair compared with the evening out. So, in general, what you can expect to be paid for providing a lunch will be much less than what you can charge for an evening meal, and the price competition will be fiercer. Whereas £25 could be charged for an evening meal with wine, most would not be prepared in Osbert's town to pay much more than £10 for lunch and are far less willing to splurge on wine. He would have to concentrate on simple table d'hôte menus as a general rule.

But there are compensations. The accountant pointed out that staff costs related to providing lunches should be lower on several counts than costs associated with evening opening. The lunch period is shorter than the evening one; daytime wages per hour are less than evening wages, especially when some of the staff will be happy to have a full-time job (even with split hours); and spare time in the evening can often be used to prepare for the next day's lunchtime custom. Similarly, spare time at lunchtime can be used to prepare for the evening's business. Moreover, if standing overheads are already to be covered by the evening meals, they do not have to be charged against the lunches as well. So the 'lunchtime' annual overheads could be reduced as shown in Table 4.6.

Table 4.6 Effect on overheads of introducing lunchtime opening

Variable overheads	£
Extra staff	35,000
Extra heating, etc	3,000
Miscellaneous	2,000
Total	40,000

On this basis Osbert would have to earn a gross profit of £40,000 ÷ 312 or £128 per day to cover these extra overheads.

Serving lunches could be made to pay if enough people came in and Osbert were able to charge about half the customers say £10, plus

£3 for a glass of wine. The accountant asked if these prices were low enough to compete with the pub lunches available at much lower costs. Osbert thought that with his restaurant's more attractive ambience and better service they could be. At these prices the gross profit per person would be £10, less VAT, less 25% = £6.38. Add £1 to cover profit on drinks, and we arrive at £7.38 per head. This means that he would need £128 ÷ 7.38 customers just to cover the extra lunchtime overheads. That means 18 people on average would have to come in each day for lunch.

Would it be worth it? Only with the 19th customer would Osbert start to make any real profit, and, the accountant asked, could he put up with the added work and worry to himself? If the overhead figures could be massaged downwards, especially in the area of staff costs, he could think again. A reduction of lunchtime overheads of £10,000 would mean that the minimum places per day would be reduced to just over 13 and profit would start to accrue with the 14th customer.

As noted in Chapter 11, the more you can convert overheads into direct (or marginal) costs, the more of a safety margin your business will have. With high overheads, overtime payments become an attractive proposition compared with taking on more permanent staff. Many restaurant proprietors are prepared to make 'stand-by' payments to part-time staff who will guarantee to come in if the place gets more than minimally busy in an evening. 'Flexi-workers' who are, within reason and for a stand-by fee, ready to surrender some leisure time and come in at short notice when needed are very valuable and well worth generous hourly pay.

After much heart-searching and discussion with his friend Guy and the accountant, Osbert decided to have a go. 'In for a penny, in for a pound.' He decided to open five days a week for lunch and to make his restaurant look as select as possible, without making it too intimidating for the more diffident customer. He paid an old college friend to make the design for him as high-Parisian in fashion as he could afford, with chandelier lighting, white linen table napery and as much sparkle as possible. Osbert had noticed that, where they were available, little booths in the old Montmartre style were very often preferred for their air of privacy and discretion. His friend filled one wall of the restaurant with them, and Osbert was delighted to find that because no room had to be left for chairs to be pulled back he could get one more table into the room than had previously been the case.

By maintaining intense pressure on the contractors for furniture, etc, Osbert avoided the hugely expensive misfortune of having to delay the opening. Luckily, the editor of the local paper came to the opening night, was pleased with what he saw and was given to eat, and gave the new venture a good write-up. The opening weeks were better than Osbert had feared, even if they were not quite as good as he had hoped for. Guy was delighted at being able to practise his art in the way he wanted, and the new waitresses, though the job was tiring, liked working in a smart and lively atmosphere. The accountant, too, was happy when the business started to show a profit – pessimistic accountants are always happy to be proved wrong!

A good start has been made and the restaurant was shown to be profitable, so far. How to keep it going? That was the question Osbert and Guy asked each other. They had seen many a fine restaurant rise and then fall away, out of fashion with its once-admiring clientele. This must not happen, at least until all the debts have been paid off and capital accumulated for an extensive relaunch or a move to another site. From Guy's point of view, that of the culinary artist, a constantly changing and expanding menu was the answer. 'Up to a point, I agree,' said Osbert, ' but I know what can happen to over-blown à la carte lists: waste and loss of control. We are fully booked most Saturday nights, and often on Fridays and Sundays too. We could have more expensive 'specials' on those nights, for instance game when in season; we could also upgrade our wine list now. Both these developments would increase our gross profit with very little effect on the overheads.'

Such are the discussions that management should have, not only in catering but in all businesses, to make sure that they do not lower their original standards and lose ground. If Osbert carries on like that, he will take some beating.

The restaurant described in this example is probably not the sort of catering establishment you would wish to run. It was not intended to be a blueprint, but a demonstration of the application of universal business principles to the running of one kind of catering enterprise. You may have very different ideas of the café or lunch-bar that you have in mind, but the principles of good business practice will still apply. Good luck to you.

5

Manufacturing

For inventors the path is hard and steep. The continuing progress of the human race depends on them, and yet often they are the last to benefit from their own ingenuity. Not all inventions or ideas are practical, but a fair proportion turn out to be commercially viable. To get them into production and sold – there's the rub!

If you are an inventor, your first priority must be to protect your invention. By all means, see a patent agent and get it registered. That is essential. But patents give very limited protection, and the registration procedure is cumbersome and expensive. Your best policy is to get production going and saturate the market fast. Once you have succeeded in that, your patent has acquired value.

As an inventor, you are faced with a choice of two basic strategies: you can adopt the 'paddle your own canoe' line, or you can sell your invention to a large concern, for a lump sum or for royalties. Either way, there are problems, and your first planning decision must be to choose between the two courses. Two examples (5.1 and 5.2) are given in this chapter to illustrate these alternatives.

An example of someone who possesses skills neither in design nor in marketing but who does have the ability to organize a production unit and can afford what is, in effect, a service to other manufacturers, is also shown (Example 5.3).

Example 5.1: Marcus Garside

This is a request for further capital to produce and test prototypes for a new automatic-car seat-belt reel. A sum of £4,000 is needed.

1. There have been continual complaints about the inconvenience of the seat-belt reels now on the market for two-door saloon cars. Much annoyance is caused to passengers entering the rear and entangling themselves in the slack of the front-seat safety belts. The problem has been to reconcile the need for a firm, reliable rewind with the safety requirements of an inertia mechanism which will hold the belt tight when the car stops suddenly. I enclose several cuttings from motoring magazines commenting on this. I have been assured that a better type of reel would have great popular appeal, and I think I have solved the problem.

2. My name is Marcus Garside. I am a trained mechanical engineer at present employed in the Quality Control Department of Bryte-look Engineering Ltd in Witherspool. In the past three years I have spent my spare time designing and making the first prototype of my new reel.

3. I enclose drawings of the design which has been tested for efficiency and reliability in three different models of car. EC patents have been obtained through Messrs Seek and Find, patent agents of Bradfield, and a US patent has been applied for. I have spent £3,500 in cash of my own money on this project to date.

4. The design is capable of improvement, now the principle has been shown to work. The design may also have to be modified for production. For both these reasons I wish to employ the services of a design engineering consultancy. The cost could well amount to £5,000, but I hope to obtain a grant of 50 per cent of this under the government Innovation Initiative Scheme. Subsequently I would want to produce a run of six prototypes, both for testing and for submission to potential buyers of my patent, the testing to be done at the Bridgeworth Engineering College or at the British Institute for Automobile Engineering. The money would be spent as shown in Table 5.1. I am able to put a further £2,500 of my own money into the project, and I am asking the Deeside County Council Enterprise Fund to lend me the additional £5,000 needed.

Table 5.1 Money to be spent on the product

	£
Consultancy (net)	2,500
Prototypes	1,000
Testing	2,000
Sundries and expenses	2,000

5. I do not intend to produce or sell this product myself. I have neither the resources nor the temperament to run a production unit of my own. It will be my object to sell the design and patent rights to a firm capable of exploiting it to the full. There are two firms in the country capable of producing the belt reel.

Example 5.2: Rosemary Rambler and Muriel Tonks

We, Rosemary Rambler and Muriel Tonks, whose business address is 14 Church Road, Witherspool PS3 7HT, are applying for a loan of £7,500 to promote the business of designing and selling garden statuary.

The market

With the increase in tourism in the United Kingdom and the need for improved and smarter hotels, gardens and parks, we have found there is a wide and expanding market for good-quality garden and hotel statues. Marble and bronze are too expensive and cast iron or mock stone lack aesthetic appeal; but the recent development by the Tolpuddle College of Advanced Technology of the new Alloy 237B has made it possible to cast statues of attractive appearance at a marketable price.

We have had one finished statue produced and maquettes made of four more. With these we have approached five hotel groups and also

40 private individuals. Great interest has been shown. Paradise View Hotels plc have given us a firm initial order for 20 statues at £650 each plus VAT and, we believe, will buy more when the initial order has been completed, ie in 12 months' time. We also have orders for four statues from private buyers.

Our sales effort so far has been limited but the results have been very encouraging. We estimate that there is a potential market for 10,000 statues of this type. We ought to be able to obtain at least 10 per cent of the market, as we are first in the field with high-quality designs and products. One thousand units sold over five years implies sales of £650,000 plus VAT.

Ourselves

Rosemary Rambler, to be artistic director and in charge of production. 1982–85: Attended the Brize-Norton College of Art. 1985–88: Worked in the atelier of Art Slivowitz, the sculptor, in Paris. 1989–90: Unemployed. 1991–96: Lecturer in Sculpture at Ourtown Polytechnic. 1996–2006: Senior Lecturer in sculpture at the University of East England. Has been commissioned to do scenery design for several theatre productions, including the famous musical *Titus Andronicus* at the London Palladium. Also designed the frieze on the new Bladderwick Town Hall.

Muriel Tonks, to be responsible for marketing and sales in addition to all office work and financial arrangements. After attending Ourtown Polytechnic classes in art for two years, went into commercial life as a management trainee at Ourtown Home Stores Ltd; at present employed there as assistant buyer. Also attending Ourtown College of Further Education classes in business management.

The product

The advantages of Alloy 237B are that the metal is both cheaper and has a lower melting point than bronze, making it easier to cast. The metal is supplied by Vintage Metals Ltd of Birmingham, and we have a contract with Stanislavski Foundry Ltd to cast two statues per month at a price to remain fixed for one year. The cost to us per standard statue, approximately 5 ft x 3 ft, including metal and casting, will be £345 plus VAT.

We shall concentrate on producing five models during the first year. Models can be ordered from maquettes as follows:

- the Copenhagen Mermaid;
- the Mannekin Pis;
- Rodin's 'Thinker';
- a lion rampant;
- a bust of Winston Churchill.

This selection was made to cater for a wide variety of tastes. Casting problems made us reject two otherwise popular suggestions, Cellini's 'Perseus' and the 'Two Ronnies'.

Our short-term plan

Our statues will be produced by what is known as the 'lost wax' method. This involves making full-size plaster models of each statue, from which the foundry can proceed to make the final metal statues.

One metal statue has been cast satisfactorily and is ready to be invoiced to the customer. Two further full-scale plaster models have been delivered to the foundry ready to be cast. Rosemary's first priority will be to complete the last two full-scale models, which, with part-time help from Muriel and some casual work from students from the College in their spare time, should take 10 weeks. In the meantime the foundry will be casting from the existing full-scale models.

We have acquired suitable premises on Church Street, Witherspool at a rent of £1,500 a year which will provide a studio for designing new models and a workshop for adding the final touches to each statue and for packing and dispatch. There is also space suitable for an office and a showroom for the display of small-scale models or maquettes.

We do not believe that, at least during the first year, we shall need to employ other than occasional casual labour.

The limiting factor is the Stanislavski Foundry's lack of sufficient capacity for casting more than one statue per fortnight. The foundry has committed itself to expansion, however, and a letter, attached hereto as Appendix A, attests to this fact.

Being essentially a marketing and design partnership, we propose to spend heavily on publicity and advertising in our first year. Muriel will concentrate on selling our products. We shall rely on mailshots, telephone sales and personal visits to large hotel groups and other likely enterprises. We propose to buy a personal computer and use it not only as a word processor for our letters, invoices, etc, but to set up a database of actual and potential customers.

We have received very useful help from the Witherspool Enterprise Agency and have gratefully accepted its offer of continuing support and advice.

We shall also consult regularly with our accountants, Messrs Belt & Braces of Ourtown.

In view of the fact that most of our customers will be commercial firms, we will register for VAT immediately.

The longer-term strategy

With a target of selling approximately 1,000 units in five years, we are planning on a rapid expansion to an annual production of 400 units in the fifth year. Such expansion will involve:

- Either a further substantial increase in capacity at the foundry we are using at present or a search for another firm able to take on the additional work.
- An increase in our range of statues by the addition of perhaps four new models a year. Market research will determine what models will be designed.
- Finding larger premises, probably in two years' time, and taking on more staff. We expect to employ three more skilled people within the five years, and at least one unskilled or semi-skilled person.

The financial situation

It has been agreed that the work already done, essentially by Rosemary, shall be valued at £4,000, this to include the one finished statue ready for sale and invoicing. A family loan to Muriel of £4,000 will be her contribution to the partnership assets. This will be paid into the partnership account on day one.

The partners will then share profits and losses equally. A partnership deed is being drawn up by Messrs Manyana, Manyana & Holliday, solicitors.

The partners are asking for a fixed-term loan of a further £4,000, repayments to start after nine months and then by eight three-month instalments. In addition, an overdraft facility of £3,500 is requested.

Of our starting capital of £8,000 we shall spend £1,500 on a small second-hand car to be used mainly for sales visits. We shall also have to equip an office and buy hoists, etc to help with packing and dispatch.

Table 5.2 shows how we plan to use the £8,000.

The need for working capital will be heavy in the first year, owing in part to the limited capacity of the foundry. Messrs Stanislavski are installing additional capacity and have promised to do their best to speed up production. In our financial forecast we have not allowed for any increase in production over what the foundry has promised to achieve. In view of our sales potential, any increase in production would have a dramatic effect on our profits and cash flow.

The following documents are attached as appendices:

Table 5.2

Car	£1,500	
Office equipment	£1,000	(including VAT)
Alterations to premises	£500	(including VAT)
Equipment	£600	(including VAT)
Working capital	£4,400	
Total	£8,000	

- letter from the Stanislavski Foundry Ltd;
- photograph of our first statue;
- schedule of overheads;
- forecasts of profit and loss and cash flow.

In these accounts we are 'capitalizing' all expenditure on design and the making of moulds. We are writing it off as a charge against the cost of each statue produced, as can be seen in the profit and loss forecast.

In our second year we expect to sell a minimum of 140 statues, producing a profit as shown in Table 5.3:

Table 5.3

	£	£
Sales		91,000
Less metal and casting	48,300	
Moulds and design	2,400	
Overheads	12,300	
Wages	7,500	
Interest	300	
Depreciation	800	71,600
Profit		19,400

A cash flow forecast was produced on the partnership's personal computer (see Table 5.4). Although it looks different from the one done on a bank form by Alexander Battersby, it does follow the basic principles laid down in Chapter 2. There, you will remember, you were advised to begin by listing all the fixed amounts you knew you would have to pay, followed by those other charges, like electricity, that would be regular but unpredictable as to the precise amount.

Rosemary and Muriel's cash flow goes beyond this by including a complete schedule of all the overhead payments they expect to make, month by month. The amounts are entered here net of VAT. Some of the items will be free of VAT and some will be subject to VAT. Next the VAT on the VATable items is calculated. At the foot of each column are added up the non-VATable items, the VATable items and the VAT thereon, the total representing the overhead payments due for the month. (The figures are shown in Table 5.4.)

You will notice a 13th column on the right which has been used to estimate the various overhead payments relevant to this year which will not be paid until after the year end. Added to the monthly payments, this will give the total of overhead expenses that affect the year's profit.

Preparing an overhead schedule like this is a useful exercise for any small business owner. If the owner knows the total commitments for overheads for a year, then by dividing by 12, he or she will know how much gross profit must be made each month just to cover the fixed overheads.

For instance, a retailer whose fixed overheads come to £12,000 a year will know that he or she must have £1,000 per month gross profit to cover them, and if his or her profit margin on sales is 25 per cent, then a turnover of £4,000 per month (nearly £200 per day) is needed for overheads alone. And this does not take into consideration any wages, any interest on capital, any depreciation or any profit for the owner.

Rosemary and Muriel also wanted to have some idea of the profit or loss they might make in their first year, so a profit and loss forecast was devised (see Table 5.5).

There is a line that represents the 'overheads', one-twelfth of the annual total excluding VAT. (Remember, if you are registered for VAT, VAT does not affect the profit and loss account.) The 'value of sales' line represents the invoiced value of the number of statues sold in the month. The 'metal and casting' figure represents the bought-in cost from the metal supplier and foundry for that same number of statues.

Rosemary and Muriel realized that in working out the cost of each statue they had to allow for the expenses incurred in making the design and in constructing the mould. They worked out the average cost per design plus mould and then divided the figure obtained by the number of statues they thought could be made from the mould before it wore out or the demand for that particular statue fell away. After careful consideration they decided on a figure of £20. One line in the profit and loss forecast represents this cost.

Table 5.4 Overhead schedule

Rosemary Rambler and Muriel Tonks

	Month 1	Month 2	Month 3	Month 4	Month 5	Month 6	Month 7	Month 8	Month 9	Month 10	Month 11	Month 12	Outstanding	Total
Rent	750						750							1,500
Rates	40	40	40	40	40	40	40	40	40	40				400
Heat and light				200			200			200			200	800
Insurance premiums (on car)	825													825
Road fund licences			200											200
Bank charges				30			30			30			30	120
Telephone	100			250			250			250			250	1,100
Advertising and printing	270	270	270	270	270	270	270	270	270	270	270	270	270	3,510
Petrol, etc	100	100	100	100	100	100	100	100	100	100	100	100		1,200
Office and other sundries	25	25	25	25	25	25	25	25	25	25	25	25		300
Professional fees		250											600	850
Repairs and renewals			100			100			100			100		400
Contingencies	30	30	30	30	30	30	30	30	30	30	30	30		360
Total (ex-VAT)	2,140	715	765	945	465	565	1,695	465	565	945	425	525	1,350	11,565
VAT thereon	92	118	92	118	74	92	118	74	92	118	74	92	96	1,250
Total payments	2,232	833	857	1,063	539	657	1,813	539	657	1,063	499	617	1,446	12,815

Table 5.5 Profit and loss and cash flow forecasts for Rosemary Rambler and Muriel Tonks

Rosemary Rambler and Muriel Tonks
Profit and loss and cash flow forecasts

Profit and loss account

	Month 1	Month 2	Month 3	Month 4	Month 5	Month 6	Month 7	Month 8	Month 9	Month 10	Month 11	Month 12	Total
Number of statues sold	1	3	3	3	4	4	4	5	5	6	6	6	50
Values of sales	650	1,950	1,950	1,950	2,600	2,600	2,600	3,250	3,250	3,900	3,900	3,900	32,500
less													
Metal and casting	285	855	855	855	1,140	1,140	1,140	1,425	1,425	1,710	1,710	1,710	14,250
Moulds and design	20	60	60	60	80	80	80	100	100	120	120	120	1,000
Overheads	964	964	964	964	964	964	964	964	964	964	964	964	11,568
Interest	47	47	47	47	47	47	47	47	47	47	47	47	564
Wages									200	200	200	200	800
Depreciation	67	67	67	67	67	67	67	67	67	67	67	67	804
Profit	−733	−43	−43	−43	302	302	302	647	447	792	792	792	3,514

Table 5.5 *continued*

	Month 1	Month 2	Month 3	Month 4	Month 5	Month 6	Month 7	Month 8	Month 9	Month 10	Month 11	Month 12	Total
Receipts from sales		764	2,291	2,291	2,291	3,055	3,055	3,055	3,819	3,819	4,583	4,583	33,605
Loans	4000												4,000
Other receipts	4000												4,000
Total receipts	8000	764	2,291	2,291	2,291	3,055	3,055	3,055	3,819	3,819	4,583	4,583	41,605
Payments for:													
Metal and casting	0	1,005	1,005	1,005	1,340	1,340	1,340	1,674	1,674	2,009	2,009	2,009	16,409
Moulding materials	453	340	0	230	230	230	230	230	230	230	230	230	2,863
Ditto wages	65	65				60	250	250	250	250	250	250	1,690
Overheads	2,232	833	857	1,063	539	657	1,813	539	657	1,063	499	617	11,370
Interest			141			141			141			123	546
Other wages									200	200	200	200	800
Drawings	500	500	500	500	500	500	500	500	500	500	500	500	6,000
Capital payments	3,600												3,600
VAT				-720			69			1,037			386
Loan repayments									500			500	1,000
Total payments	6,850	2,743	2,503	2,077	2,609	2,927	4,202	3,194	4,152	5,289	3,689	4,429	44,664
Balance	1,150	-1,979	-211	214	-318	128	-1,147	-139	-334	-1,471	894	153	-3,059
Bank balance	1,150	-829	-1,040	-826	-1,144	-1,016	-2,163	-2,302	-2,636	-4,106	-3,212	-3,059	-3,059

There is also a line for 'interest' payable on their loan. And a line for 'wages' – other than wages for design and mould making, which are included in the £20. Other than for making moulds, they do not expect to have to employ anyone during the first year.

The last item of expenditure is 'depreciation'.

Next, Muriel prepared a cash flow forecast for the year. In this table all figures must include VAT, where applicable, as she is dealing with the actual movement of cash. The 'receipts from sales' line represents the actual money received for the statues assuming they were paid for in the month after they were invoiced.

The 'moulding materials and wages' represent the amounts actually spent on these items, as do the amounts for 'overheads' – from the 'overhead schedule' – for 'interest' and for 'capital payments'.

There is a line for 'drawings' representing what Rosemary and Muriel need as living expenses, and lines to show the cash they have borrowed and their own money which they have introduced. The 'loan repayments' are also shown in their due time.

The VAT line is constructed by deducting the VAT on payments to suppliers, both of ongoing costs and overheads, and the capital payments, from the VAT charge to customers. The calculation is made quarterly, and payment is made in the month immediately after the quarter's end.

Note that, owing to the heavy payments combined with a lack of receipts in the first month, Rosemary and Muriel will be able to claim a VAT repayment for the first quarter.

Next, let us consider a team which has a patent and, believing its product to be a commercial proposition, wishes to produce and market it as well. The combination of two men or women, both in the same line of business, one with marketing, the other with production skills, will obviously be stronger than either alone, and they have been wise enough to invite a colleague to join them, albeit part-time, a man with the financial knowledge and skills to keep them in line over their cash problems. They have also agreed that their main aim in the first year will be to set up an efficient production system.

Although the managing director will pay a great deal of attention to the marketing of their products, they have decided to defer setting up their own selling organization for the time being and to rely on sales through another firm. Time will tell whether the strategy will pay off, but at least it gives a management limited in number a chance to succeed.

Example 5.3: James Turbotte, Brian Fletcher and Julian Watchman

This is a project to manufacture left-handed snooker cues for which we have identified an expanding market. We need additional finance of £50,000.

Our market

The Snooker Cue Maker Society's annual report for 2007 gives the total number of cues sold in the period September 2006–August 2007 as 200,000. All the major cue makers make only right-handed cues.

Published figures (HMSO Statistics of Handedness) show that 7.8 per cent of males aged between 10 and 60 are left-handed to the extent that they have difficulty in using right-handed tools.

A sample survey of 452 interviews with left-handed men showed that:

- 72 per cent did not want to play snooker;
- 10 per cent would play if left-handed cues were available;
- 7 per cent played with right-handed cues without difficulty;
- 9 per cent played with right-handed cues with great difficulty;
- 2 per cent refused to answer.

From the above figures we have deduced that there is a potential market for between 50,000 and 80,000 left-handed cues per annum.

We interviewed Hector McWhirter, the 2000 St Kilda and Rockall Snooker Champion, who is known to be left-handed. Mr McWhirter uses a custom-made left-handed cue. He told us that until he had such a cue specially made, he was 'getting nowhere'. He said that the new cue had added 25 points per frame to his game. Mr McWhirter has offered to sponsor our venture but would expect a small fee.

Three main agents distribute 55 per cent of snooker cues, and 45 per cent are sold directly through the normal retail channels. We have decided, in view of our limited sales and distribution facilities, to sell through the leading agents. Galligaskin and Breeks Ltd have agreed to place an initial order of 1,000 and to join with us in a sales and publicity campaign.

The directors

James Turbotte is the founder of the company. Since leaving school all his career has been spent in the sports goods industry:

1982–88	Trainee at Consolidated Cricket Bats Ltd
1988–94	Salesman for Hurry & Push Ltd in their Sports Goods Department
1994–99	Assistant sales manager, Potpink Ltd
1999–2006	Sales manager, Potpink Ltd.

In 2006 Potpink Ltd was taken over by Sportsell Inc, so in December 2006 Turbotte was made redundant. Since then, in conjunction with Brian Fletcher, he has been developing the new left-handed cue and doing the necessary market research. He thinks he can claim that nobody knows the snooker cue market better than he does. He has invested his savings of £10,500 in the company and has taken out a second mortgage on his house to raise a further £24,000.

Brian Fletcher holds the City and Guilds Certificate (Grade 4) in Snooker Cue Making. He has spent all his working life in the Cue Department of Potpink Ltd. For three years he was manager in charge of technical developments. He too was made redundant when Sportsell transferred production to Korea in 2006. He has helped to design the new cue and will be production director. By remortgaging his house, he has raised £10,500 to invest in the company.

Julian Watchman is a chartered accountant. He is employed by a local firm of accountants but has been given permission by them to serve on the company's board as financial director. He has borrowed £12,500 from family sources to invest in the company.

Auditors: Messrs Belt & Braces, Queen Street, Ourtown

Solicitors: Messrs Manyana, Manyana & Holliday

The product

Our cue has been designed for left-handed players by realigning the grip at the butt end, by adjusting the torque in the shaft, and by using a special tip invented by Brian Fletcher (EC Patent No 158692). This allows a left-handed player the same freedom of arm action as his right-handed rival. Independent tests (see below) have shown that:

- grip realignment alone has improved accuracy in the cue ball by 7.13 per cent and the accuracy of path of the object ball by 6.78 per cent;
- torque adjustment alone has improved accuracy in the cue ball by 2.38 per cent and path accuracy of the object ball by 2.86 per cent;
- the new tip (the Accutip) alone improved cue ball accuracy by 11.29 per cent and object ball accuracy by 13.17 per cent;
- the overall improvement in accuracy, using all three together, was cue ball, 18.72 per cent; object ball, 19.98 per cent;
- technical experts tell us that 'counter-compensation' accounts for the total improvement being less than the sum of the individual gains.

We intend to take advantage of the skill and experience of Brian Fletcher to manufacture the cues ourselves, but we propose to subcontract out the final lacquering and painting.

We have selected the necessary machinery, and the special tools have been designed. By using good second-hand equipment, we should not have to spend more than £46,000 in all on machinery and tools.

Costings based on quotations received, and the best possible estimates at the time of going to press, indicate an ex-works cost per cue of approximately £16. Galligaskin and Breeks, on their initial order, have contracted to pay £30 per cue, leaving £14 to cover overheads and profit. (See financial forecast appended.)

Our cues, therefore, should sell in the shops at a price of £70 each. This is about 8 per cent more than the price of a 'Championship' standard right-handed cue, but we believe that the increased efficiency of our product for left-handers will more than compensate for this and allow us to prosper in the market.

The Snooker Players Association was good enough to arrange for independent testing of the cue. The results, summarized above, are set out in Appendix 2.

Our short-term strategy

With our limited resources of both workforce and money, we cannot have, at this stage, a marketing policy that involves our own sales force and distributional system. For that reason we have entered into a contract, for one year, with Galligaskin and Breeks Ltd of London, under which they will market our product on an exclusive basis. They have undertaken to place an initial contract for not less than 5,000 cues. Galligaskin and Breeks have agreed to meet 50 per cent of advertising and publicity costs for the launch up to an agreed sum.

We have planned a publicity and advertising campaign with emphasis on a presence at all major tournaments during the next year in the United Kingdom.

James Turbotte will be responsible for all marketing and also the overall day-to-day control.

Brian Fletcher will manage all production, purchasing and transport. He will be aided by an assistant manager who will have special responsibility for quality control.

Julian Watchman will be a non-executive director but will attend the weekly management meetings we intend to hold and will oversee the finances of the company. An office manager has been appointed.

Suitable premises have been acquired on a seven-year lease in the old Copperbottom Mill, Ourtown. We move in on 1 October.

Secondhand machinery of excellent quality is obtainable, save that we shall have to have a special tool to our own design made by Drop-forge and Lathe of Milston. Designs for this tool have been agreed. Delivery is promised by 1 October.

Very favourable terms have been quoted for the final lacquering and painting, which is being subcontracted out, by at least two firms of repute.

Four skilled cue-makers have been recruited and, with five unskilled persons, should suffice for production of up to 350 cues per week. We envisage a total work force of 14 persons other than the directors. Each additional quantity of 100 cues per week will mean an increase in staff, which we will meet through a training programme. We believe that the machinery and equipment which we have or propose to buy will cover production needs of up to 750 cues per week. The premises are adequate for up to 1,000 cues per week.

Our office manager is an experienced bookkeeper. We intend to run a full set of weekly management accounts, together with a daily update, for the managing director, of cash, debtors, orders on hand, etc. Our books will be kept manually for the time being, but a small personal computer is available for the customer database and other management uses.

Our long-term strategy

The sports goods market is highly competitive, especially for games that are as popular and widely played as snooker. Our patents will give us some protection, but we believe that our long-term success will depend on our building up a very high share of the market.

Our five-year strategy, therefore, will be as follows:

1. To build up, in the first year, an expandable production capacity.
2. To build in, at the same time, reliable systems of quality control. We are engaging Krishman-Davis Associates as consultants in this field and are applying for a Department of Trade and Industry grant to enable us to pay their fees.

3. To investigate the market opportunities both in the UK and overseas.

4. In the second and subsequent years, to create our own company sales and marketing division to exploit any additional markets.

5. To develop the Accutip for use in standard right-handed cues. Whether we shall extend our manufacturing to include making right-handed cues ourselves, or whether we shall license the Accutip to other manufacturers, will depend on the market conditions and resources available at the time.

6. To keep our eyes open for the acquisition of any company whose business would support or enhance the production or sale of our product. We should not, however, allow the purchase of such a company to divert resources from our main objective.

We fully intend to be a major force in our own market within a five-year period. The rapid expansion envisaged makes it unlikely that any cash will be available for the payment of dividends within the five-year period.

Financial requirements

We are seeking a loan, under the Small Firms Loan Guarantee Scheme, of £50,000. Additional capital of £40,000 is being subscribed by the directors to make a total ordinary share capital of £57,000 as shown in Table 5.6.

Table 5.6 Total ordinary share capital

	£
James Turbotte	34,500
Brian Fletcher	10,500
Julian Watchman	12,500
	£57,500

The additional capital will be used as shown in Table 5.7.

Table 5.7   Additional capital

	£
Plant and machinery	46,000
Office equipment	6,000
Personal computer and software	5,000
Sundry start-up costs	2,000
Working capital	31,000
	£90,000

Two motor cars and a van are being acquired under a leasing arrangement.

Financial expectations

We are enclosing, as Appendix 4, a financial business model drawn up for us by Messrs Belt & Braces.

We have a sales target of 16,500 cues for the first 12 months. Based on this, our profit and loss account for the year will be as shown in Table 5.8.

Table 5.8   Profit and loss account for the first year

	£	£
Sales		500,000
less establishment costs (rent, fuel, etc)	60,000	
Directors' fees	41,000	
Office and administration	27,000	
Professional fees	15,000	
Advertising and publicity	30,000	
Sundries and contingency	10,000	
Interest payable	5,000	
Depreciation	17,500	
	205,500	
Wages and materials	270,000	
Sub-contracting	50,000	525,500
Net loss for the year		25,500

Table 5.9 Profit and loss account for the second year

	£	£
Sales		1,000,000
less establishment costs (rent, fuel, etc)	62,500	
Directors' fees	41,000	
Office and administration	30,000	
Professional fees	10,000	
Advertising and publicity	45,000	
Sundries and contingency	10,000	
Interest payable	2,000	
Depreciation	17,500	
	218,000	
Wages and materials	540,000	
Sub-contracting	100,000	858,000
Net profit for the year		142,000

The intention is to double sales and production in the second year. With a turnover of £1 million per annum (33,500 cues), our profit and loss account should be as shown in Table 5.9.

Under their service contracts, the two working directors, James Turbotte and Brian Fletcher, are entitled to a bonus of 5 per cent on all net profit over £20,000. Their bonus for the second year, on the above forecast, would be £6,100 each.

We are enclosing the following appendices:

1. Market survey figures of left-handed snooker players.
2. Test results from Snooker Players Association.
3. Copy of agreement for one year with Galligaskin and Breeks Ltd.
4. Financial forecasts produced by Messrs Belt & Braces.
5. Service contracts for each director.

6

Expanding a business

One need hardly point out that it is easier to obtain funds to expand an existing business than to get money to start one from scratch, assuming the business has been reasonably successful. Raising money to rescue an ailing business is at least as difficult as obtaining it for a start-up. This chapter deals with the expansion of businesses with a fair track record.

There are three good, obvious reasons that money for expansion is easier to come by than finance for a brand new business:

▪ the fact that there is a market for your product or service has already been demonstrated;
▪ you and your team have shown yourselves capable of running a business, at least so far;
▪ the business is already profitable.

One other advantage is that you know, from first-hand experience, what is going on in your business, what the problems are and what are the real possibilities. This will be apparent and inspire confidence, provided your plan for expansion is clearly presented.

In writing your plan, you will start, of course with a brief history of your business, what it has done, what it is doing, the difficulties it has faced and overcome, and the problems and opportunities it now has to solve or exploit and for which the money is needed. A brief schedule of the turnover and profits of the past few years will refer to fuller accounts and balance sheets in your first appendix.

Although you have established that you have a satisfactory market, you still have to convince your reader that the market is big enough to absorb the products of your expansion or that the new markets you hope to penetrate will be receptive to your goods or services. As you will have been listening to your customers' feedback of comment and continuing your market research and exploration, this should not be too difficult.

The section on management is another matter. When you wrote your first or start-up business plan, you had to sell yourself as a manager, and personal details mattered. Now you have proved yourself, at least as far as running your business at its present size is concerned. However, on the assumption that you are requiring finance for a significant increase in output, your business will be seen as about to enter a new phase, in which the old patterns and methods of management may well have to change.

For example, up to now, if there was a production crisis, you could call for more overtime from the team, take off your jacket, sit down at the bench and solve the problems by your own efforts. If next week looked bad for orders, a few phone calls one morning might well work wonders. Or, if there was a short-fall of cash, you could draw out less for yourself for a week or two, postpone the odd payment or ring up a big debtor and cajole a payment out of him or her. As your business gets bigger, this style of 'crisis management' just will not work as it did.

As you will remember, it was argued in Chapter 5 that it takes an exceptional genius to maintain detailed control of a business above a certain level. It may be that you will not reach that level, even with the planned expansion. Perhaps the employment of a competent works foreman/woman, the installation of a good management accounting system and the help, when needed, of the local Enterprise Agency will see you through. There is no need to over-elaborate a management system. But there are situations where, perhaps through the temperament of the main entrepreneur, proper management controls are essential, and an account of one such case is included.

However, experience does show that when a substantial amount of new money is needed for expansion, the business will also need a change of management style and an infusion of supplementary management skills. Some venture capital firms even insist on introducing some of their own management skills, almost always financial control, into the business in which they are investing. The management system is very important, and it is worth spending time and effort to convince the readers of your plan that you recognize the problem and have a management strategy which is balanced and will work.

There are two other sections of your business plan that will require special attention when money is sought for expansion. In the Introduction, four ways of achieving success in a competitive world were suggested:

- innovation;
- cheaper products;
- better service;
- better quality of goods.

Expansion means moving out into a world where you hope to be a bigger fish in a bigger pond. Your choice from the above alternative strategies becomes more crucial. When you write your plan you must make clear which strategy or strategies you are choosing and show that you understand the management consequences of your decision. For instance, if 'innovation' is your choice, in order to maintain progress the money you plough back into the business should go largely into research and development.

If you choose the 'cheaper product' line of action – which can be very dangerous for a small business – your policy must be to minimize overheads and to keep the marginal cost of production as low as possible.

'Better service' involves top managerial attention to matters such as delivery dates, after-sales visits to customers or clients, a financial policy with relatively high overheads and high profit margins.

'Better quality of goods' commits you to a high degree of design innovation and the strictest quality control. Make sure that the section or the business plan labelled 'strategy' or 'the longer-term view' shows your tactics and management to be in harmony with the overall strategy.

You must also give special attention to the part of your plan that deals with the use to which you intend to put the money you are seeking. Do ask for a large enough sum, more even than you think you will need. You may have heard the story of the bank manager who, when asked for a loan of £30,000, automatically offered £20,000 (secured, or course); then, when his customer failed for lack of sufficient capital, congratulated himself on having prevented the man from losing £10,000 more! It is to be hoped that this type of bank manager is now extinct. However, you would be wise to make sure that you are not under-capitalized. Ask for plenty. You may need it for a crisis you cannot foresee. If you are offered less, don't be afraid to turn it down!

The section on finance will be of special importance to your lender(s). It is here that they will expect to find out what is in the deal for themselves. You may be able to raise the equity through the Enterprise Investment Scheme (EIS). In this section you must explain, as fully as you can, how your backers will get their reward for entrusting their money to you for your business.

Three examples will serve to illustrate this chapter. The first is a very simple application for funds to carry out further work on a canal-side marina, and involves neither marketing nor management problems. The second is an approach by an imaginary technological company trying to raise money for the manufacture of an imaginary product. The commercial aspects will be dealt with here. The third shows that expansion can expose flaws in management that need drastic measures to overcome them.

In the case of the marina, a simple cash flow forecast, such as could be produced by the owner, is appended (Table 6.2, page 100). In the case of the high-tech manufacturer, the financial modelling and projections could be the responsibility of a specialist accountant. The problems of organization are concentrated on and no attempt is made to give financial forecasts of either profit and loss or cash flow.

Example 6.1: John S Brook

The Wagbatch Marina Ltd is seeking a loan of £25,000 to finance the second stage of the marina project at Wagbatch on the Dove and Derwent Canal.

History

I, John S Brook, having some time ago inherited 20 acres of land immediately adjoining the Dove and Derwent Canal, was made redundant by the Megapolitan Engineering Company plc in 1999. I used £20,000 of my redundancy money to form a company to excavate and develop a 45-berth marina for canal boats, which was completed in the late summer of 2000. Such was the demand that the company was able to let 30 berths to overwintering craft, and the whole marina was full during the summer of 2002 and continued to be so through 2002–07.

The company also runs a Calor gas supply service to the boat owners (and others), and in the summer opened a small shop to supply the passing trade.

As will be seen from the enclosed accounts (Appendix A), mooring fees amounted to £15,000 during the first year to 30 September 2002, gas sales to £1,087, and shop sales to £3,963. The profit, after payment of all expenses, amounted to £1,017.

The market

The use of the English canals and waterways for pleasure boating, whether by traditional style 7-foot wide longboats or by smaller cruisers, has been increasing by 5 per cent a year over the past few years and shows no sign of decreasing. More derelict canals are being brought back into use by the joint efforts of volunteer enthusiasts and the British Waterways Board. With increasing numbers of boats on the water, the demand for permanent berths in off-canal marinas exceeds the places available. The company regularly has to turn away applicants for berths.

There is also an increasing demand for other facilities, ie canalside shopping for the summer boat users, and Calor gas, especially during the colder months, etc. The company has considered the provision of diesel fuel for the boats but as yet is not convinced of the profitability.

Sales and service

The company charges 65p plus VAT per foot-length of boat per month under six-monthly contracts. Boats can range in length from about 24 to 70 ft, with a mean length of 30 ft. This gives an annual rental per boat of £234 plus VAT.

The company has an arrangement with the British Waterways Board whereby the annual BWB licence fee is collected from the boat owners and paid over to the BWB, less a collecting discount of 5 per cent. Other sources of income are the profits from the sale of Calor gas and from the shop sales.

A rental of £4,500 per annum is paid to the Waterways Board for the access to the canal itself.

What the company will do

The company will excavate and line with concrete an extension to the existing marina. The work will be relatively easy because no additional access to the canal is required and because the level of the canal itself is 3 ft higher than the average height of the area to be excavated.

The company has a provisional contract with Reilly Contractors for the construction. It will supply earth-moving equipment, shuttering and labour, and Wagbatch will supply materials. Plans have been drawn up by C Wren and Associates, the architects, and approved by the local authority. It is hoped that the work will be completed during September, in time for over-winter letting, beginning in October.

The extra rental fees to be obtained per year are estimated to be in the region of £10,000 plus VAT. As the extra annual costs involved in these rentals are small, the increase in annual profit will be close to this extra rental.

Long-term plans

The object of the enterprise is to provide me with a long-term income for my semi-retirement and for later years. There are plans to extend the marina to a total of 100 berths. Plans are also in hand for the leasing of part of the land for a boat repairing yard. The person who would run this yard is negotiating with the Rural Development Commission for financial and other support. Eventually the shop is to be let, and possibly also the Calor gas sales business.

By the time I reach normal retirement age, I hope to have completed all this. There should be a rental income to me of £25,000. See Tables 6.1 and 6.2 for cash flow forecasts.

For the first year it will be seen that, apart from the capital expenditure, there is likely to be a cash surplus of over £6,000 (£22,000 – £16,000). In the following year, when the benefits of the projected extension come through, the cash surplus increases to £20,000.

I do not need to draw any money for myself out of the enterprise during this two-year period as, for the time being, I have other income resources.

Table 6.1 John S Brook's cash flow forecast year 1

Wagbatch Marina

	Oct	Nov	Dec	Jan	Feb	Mar	Apr	May	Jun	Jul	Aug	Sept	Total
Moorings (no)	4	35	4	2	0	0	2	37	5	1	0	0	0
Mooring rents	100	550	4,812	550	275	0	0	275	5,087	687	137	0	12,373
Licences	100	100	0	0	100	130	130	130	130	130	130	100	1,180
Sales – gas	102	189	197	213	184	225	210	190	90	20	20	100	1,740
Sales – shop	0	0	0	0	0	0	255	715	766	1,277	1,788	715	5,517
Total revenue	202	839	5,009	763	559	355	595	1,310	6,073	2,115	2,075	915	20,810
Licences	0	95	95	0	0	95	124	124	124	124	124	124	1,029
Purchases – gas	85	161	167	181	156	191	179	162	77	17	17	85	1,478
Purchases – shop	0	0	0	0	0	0	460	556	766	1,149	939	269	4,139
Rent BWB			1,125			1,125			1,125			1,125	4,500
Rates	50	50	50	50			52	52	52	52	52	52	512
Insurance	125												125
Repairs								153	153	153			459
Professional fees						705							705
Interest			82			31			78				191
Capital payments									1,175	7,050	7,050	7,050	22,325
VAT payable	27			871			215			431			1,544
Total payments	287	306	1,519	1,102	156	2,147	1,030	1,047	3,550	8,976	8,182	8,705	37,007
Cash flow	–85	533	3,490	–339	403	–1,792	–435	263	2,523	–6,861	–6,107	–7,790	–16,197
Opening bank	–3,215	–3,300	–2,767	723	384	787	–1,005	–1,440	–1,177	1,346	–5,515	–11,622	
Closing bank	–3,300	–2,767	723	384	787	–1,005	–1,440	–1,177	1,346	–5,515	–11,622	–19,412	

Table 6.2 John S Brook's cash flow forecast year 2

Wagbatch Marina

	Oct	Nov	Dec	Jan	Feb	Mar	Apr	May	Jun	Jul	Aug	Sept	Total
Moorings (no)	20	53	15	7	0	0	20	53	15	7	0	0	190
Mooring rents	0	2,750	7,286	2,062	962	0	0	2,750	7,286	2,062	962	0	26,120
Licences	200	200	0	0	190	250	250	250	260	250	240	190	2,280
Sales – gas	200	300	350	375	350	425	425	350	175	50	20	100	3,120
Sales – shop	0	0	0	0	0	0	360	900	950	1,500	2,600	1,000	7,310
Total revenue	400	3,250	7,636	2,437	1,502	675	1,035	4,250	8,671	3,862	3,822	1,290	38,830
Licences	0	95	95	0	0	95	124	124	124	124	124	124	1,029
Purchases – gas	85	255	298	319	298	361	361	298	149	43	17	85	2,669
Purchases – shop	0	0	0	0	0	0	600	680	900	1,450	1,325	375	5,330
Rent BWB			1,125			1,125			1,125			1,125	4,500
Rates	52	52	52	52			55	55	55	55	55	55	538
Insurance	250												250
Repairs							250	250	250				750
Professional fees						690							690
Interest						460			500			235	1,811
Capital payments	1,150												1,150
VAT payable	−2,242		616	1,450			622			1,311			1,141
Total payments	−705	402	2,186	1,821	298	2,731	2,012	1,407	3,103	2,983	1,521	1,999	19,758
Cash flow	1,105	2,848	5,450	616	1,204	−2,056	−977	2,843	5,568	879	2,301	−709	19,072
Opening bank	−19,412	−18,307	−15,459	−10,009	−9,393	−8,189	−10,245	−11,222	−8,379	−2,811	−1,932	−369	−19,412
Closing bank	−18,307	−15,459	−10,009	−9,393	−8,189	−10,245	−11,222	−8,379	−2,811	−1,932	−369	−340	−340

Example 6.2: Kenneth Jackson Allen and Anthony Kevin Spooner

Note: the following example is not intended as a description of a possible technical proposition but to show how such a proposition might be planned and presented.

Bradfield Tectonics Ltd

The above company is seeking further capital of £100,000 to increase production of its seismic detection apparatus.

History

Bradfield Tectonics Ltd was formed in 2000 with a capital of 1,000 shares of £1 each. 900 of these shares are held by the managing director, K J Allen, BA (Cantab), PhD (London), and the other 100 by Professor Boothaway of the Department of Geophysics at Bradfield University.

The company's objective was to develop an improved seismic detector, as specified by Professor Boothaway. His work on the local geological feature known as the Duffton fault, and later on the far more active Santa Isabel fault in Mexico, is well known. His research in this field persuaded him of the need for a more sensitive seismic detector, encompassing, if possible, some directional capability.

The problem was referred to Dr Allen, at that time Reader in Scientific Instrumentation at Calderwood University. Dr Allen produced a solution to the problem, and in 2000 the company was formed to develop the project and produce the instrument concerned.

Research and development in the first year was funded in part by a loan of £10,000 from Dr Allen (convertible at any time into ordinary shares in the company at par value), in part by a government research grant, and in part by Bradfield University in return for an option to subscribe for 20 per cent of the company's ordinary shares at any time before 31 December 2007, at par or net asset value per share, whichever is the greater.

The accounts for the two years ended 30 September 2002 are enclosed as Appendix A. There was no production in the first year, which showed a loss of £9,237. In the second year six instruments were completed and sold (all for export) at an ex-works price of £32,000 each. This produced a tiny net profit for the year of £789. The staff then consisted of Dr Allen himself, an electronics production engineer and two workmen, one skilled, one semi-skilled. The company concentrated on assembly and quality assurance, relying on sub-contractors for parts and sub-assemblies.

Enclosed is an account by Professor Boothaway of the geophysical principles and technicalities involved (Appendix B).

The market

On 1 October 2002 the company had an order book for 10 instruments, together with virtually certain orders for a further 12. Steps had already been taken to increase production capacity, both in consultation with the company's suppliers and its own training programme. At that time the market situation was transformed because of a paper read by Professor Wu of the Wei University, China, at the International Seismological Conference held in Djakarta in September 2002. The subject of Professor Wu's paper was 'Predictive uses of small earth movements', which demonstrated how the profile of small earth movements could be used to predict earthquakes of Richter Scale 5 or more, provided the data were sufficiently accurate as to scale and location. The instrument that Bradfield Tectonics is producing is the only one capable of this accuracy at present on the market.

Visits undertaken by Professor Boothaway to the authorities in Japan and California have produced letters of intent for the purchase of 80 instruments. The directors are satisfied that a wide and expanding demand for the product exists in all areas of the world where earthquakes can be expected.

The directors

Kenneth Jackson Allen, managing director. Dr Allen obtained first-class honours in physics at Cambridge in 1988. He obtained a PhD for research at the Imperial College of Science in 1990. From 1990 to 1999 he was with Faraday Electric plc, eventually becoming marketing controller for the Instruments Division. In 1999 he was offered the post of Reader in Scientific Instrumentation at Calderwood. He resigned his readership in 2000 to set up Bradfield Tectonics.

Anthony Kevin Spooner, BSc (London). Anthony Spooner obtained a degree in physics. He is also a member of the Institute of Electrical Engineers. A former junior colleague of Dr Allen at Faraday Electric plc, Anthony was offered, in 1998, a position with Supersonic Instruments Inc, becoming production manager at that company's plant in Columbus, Ohio, in 2000. The challenge of the new product lured him back to England. He will take up the position of production director when his contract with Supersonic ends in two months' time.

The company's accountants are Smith, Brodsky and Toole, 6 Lomas Street, Bradfield.

The company's solicitors are Fifield and Partners, Sepulchre Chambers, Bradfield.

The product

Appendix C contains a full description of the product and its technological specifications. Essentially it consists of three highly sensitive earth tremor detectors to be located approximately 500 metres apart and connected by cable. Of the three stations, one, the master station, is equipped with sufficient microchip software to correlate the data from all the detectors and to locate, by triangulation, the epicentre of the disturbance.

Our instruments have so far been placed near inhabited areas but it is highly desirable for them to be placed also in very remote situations. We, in conjunction with the university, are developing a) a solar cell system to provide the necessary power and b) an internet/mobile phone communications system between the individual stations and the central organization. We are budgeting for the cost of this.

Short-term policy

So far production has been carried out in a small workshop under the Sheltered Workshop Scheme operated by Bradfield City Council. Already the accommodation has proved to be utterly inadequate. The company has arranged to buy the lease on a factory on the Enterprise Estate, Witherspool, which should prove large enough to meet requirements for some time to come.

The recruitment and training of staff will be of vital importance. The production engineer employed at present is young and his experience is limited, but he is keen and capable, and the company proposes to send him on a course and promote him to assembly shop manager. Four more production workers will be needed, and these will be trained by the company, a training grant having been negotiated with the county council.

The next problem will be the recruitment of service engineers. The company offers its customers a maintenance contract. Maintenance is bound to be expensive because of the travelling involved, and so a substantial margin is being built into the company's costings to cover after-sales service and contingencies. The sums are credited to a 'Maintenance and Service Reserve', and this will be debited with any service charges or fault claims exceeding the fees charged for maintenance. To date, what little maintenance has been required has been carried out by Dr Allen himself and combined with sales visits to potential clients. However, for the future two service engineers willing to travel wherever needed are being recruited and trained.

A chartered or certified accountant to take charge of the financial side is also being recruited. A personal computer is being acquired on which to keep the accounts. It will also carry a database of all customers and potential customers, as well as a record of units sold, together with all the information concerning the performance of each instrument.

Bradfield University will make one of its own computers available for all computer assisted design work and computer assisted manufacturing.

Long-term strategy

At present the company is very much a one-product organization. The sudden opening-up of the market means that in the short term the policy must be to exploit this opportunity to its full extent. The company's production plans and marketing drive have had to be brought forward; hence the present demand for capital.

Bradfield Tectonics Ltd enjoys a special relationship with the Bradfield University Department of Geophysics, and in the longer term the company's aim is to become research-based. Its expertise will be in instrumentation, and its budgeting for the future envisages applying 10 per cent, at least, of gross turnover to Research and Development.

Financial considerations

Dr Allen and Professor Boothaway together will subscribe for a further 29,000 ordinary shares, pro rata to their existing holdings. Anthony Spooner has agreed to invest £25,000 in the company for a 25 per cent shareholding, ie 10,000 shares, at a price of £2.50 each. Accordingly, the share capital will be as shown in Table 6.3.

Table 6.3   Share capital

			£
Dr Allen	27,000	shares	27,000
Professor Boothaway	3,000	shares	3,000
A Spooner	10,000	shares	10,000
Share premium account			15,000
Shareholders' funds			£55,000

The company is seeking to raise a further £100,000 in long-term finance, either by a loan, convertible loan stock, or by means of a mixed issue of loan and equity.

The additional funds will be used as shown in Table 6.4.

Table 6.4   Use of additional funds

	£
Premium on lease	20,000
Machinery and test equipment	50,000
Office equipment and computer	15,000
Motor cars	20,000
Working capital	49,000
Immediately needed research	30,000
	£184,000

Dr Allen and A Spooner will receive a salary of £25,000 a year each, plus bonuses on profits and share options as set out in the draft service agreements (Appendix D).

Profit and loss, cash flow, and balance sheet forecast are enclosed (Appendix E).

The third example of the need for a thorough re-planning has the financial aspect only in the background. A sound capitalization is essential, of course, but a functioning management set-up is almost as important. As in most walks of life, especially sport, a team of mutual admiring mediocrities will triumph over a gang of squabbling and disorganized geniuses.

Example 6.3: George Weston

George Weston has a round pink face and a perpetual good-natured expression. His eyes never narrow and he never makes an impatient gesture. All this helps to make him a first-class salesman. He also knows his stuff. His training as an electronic engineer was sound and thorough. So well absorbed indeed was his knowledge that he was able to get his technology over to anyone. To the expert he was convincing and to the person who had to sign the cheque he could explain himself using only that amount of jargon that made the signatory feel that he or she was not being talked down to.

Leonard, his first partner, was a very different type. Leonard had no time for anyone who could not understand the technical terms and engineering calculations that increasingly replaced the English language in his mind. He was a design engineer of very considerable talent but of a somewhat sour disposition, and anyone who has had dealings with such a person will know how difficult Leonard could be.

George had decided that the world could be sold an improved loudspeaker for public address purposes, a speaker that allowed for the fact that elderly people going a little deaf lost the higher notes before the lower ones and so found certain consonants impossible to hear. Leonard was the expert he found who could work out how the problem could be solved. Between them solve it they did. George began to sell the first new systems and they employed a skilled mechanic (Bill Batty) to get the things actually made.

Bill Batty had come up through the apprenticeship system which made him a very skilled 'man of his hands' and extraordinarily capable of rising to the occasion and dealing with a crisis. But he had never been in charge of a workshop before and was not methodical in the housekeeping side of his job. Parts were not ordered in time and so on, and he did not keep the flow of work to the operatives steady and even. He tried to compensate for these deficiencies by superhuman personal efforts. Needless to say he and Leonard were forever at odds.

It is the way of imaginative design engineers never to be satisfied. So it was with Leonard. He was forever making improvements. Never did a final design get approved. Money was being lost while he fussed over his brainchild and insisted on 'one more essential' modification. In the end George could stand it no longer and after a furious quarrel he offered to buy Leonard out. Leonard fought hard to keep control of what he considered his own invention, but at last the deal was done. George mortgaged his house and borrowed from his brother and set out on his own. Leonard joined a firm of competitors but

George had had the basic sense to register all patents in the firm's name.

George now sought the advice of an experienced local accountant as to how he should restructure his business. It was decided that George would need a production manager, and it was hoped that Bill Batty would do, with the help of a new quality assurance controller. A young, recently qualified engineer was engaged to do such design modifications as would become necessary, and would deal with any problems those customers found with the firm's installations. The accountant insisted that George's role should be that of overall management, and he should spend less of his own time outside doing the selling and more inside the office overseeing everything.

So George hired an engineer-salesman; but the choice of Duncan McTaggart was the source of the future troubles. Duncan had a weakness that was common among travelling salesmen. His status among his fellow travellers that he met and talked to in hotels, and his own ego, was bound up with the car he drove. He negotiated with George that he should have a BMW, and was even prepared to receive a lower salary and bonus to get one. When Mrs McTaggart found out about the terms of her husband's job she was furious that money that should have been used for her children's benefit was going simply to feed Duncan's self-esteem. So she gave him a hard time, which made him resentful, too.

Millicent, George's own wife, was also disgruntled over this matter. She was already dissatisfied with the way things were going. For all her husband's hard work, and the support she gave him, money was not coming in; in fact the debts were increasing, and she was feeling insecure. And here was this underling getting a snazzy car while she, the boss's wife, had to put up with a five-year-old Ford. George did his best to soothe her with words of hope for the future, but in the end had to agree to buy a BMW, and a more expensive model, for himself. He told Millicent that he was doing it 'through the business' but that was eyewash. It added to the large debt that was ultimately his responsibility, and the cost of two BMWs were a significant factor in all his subsequent troubles.

McTaggart, though a determined and even aggressive character, was unfortunately also lazy. Even with his BMW to show off, spending his time going from potential customer to potential customer in, say, Newcastle-on-Tyne in November was not to his taste even if he was being paid for it. He preferred to sit in a warm office and make telephone calls. George was depressed by his attitude and the fact that sales opportunities were being lost. However, George's own good nature, and the intimidating attitude McTaggart could adopt, worked against the obvious solution.

The product was nevertheless a success and George ventured over to Spain where he had connections and obtained two very substantial orders by his own efforts. Now most firms find a steady stream of small orders much easier to manage than sudden large orders, glamorous though the latter may be. So these two jumbo-sized orders created management problems.

Different members of the staff reacted differently. Bill Batty grumbled, swore the orders could never be fulfilled in time and threatened to resign, but secretly he found it an exciting and desperate challenge. He could not control his stock of materials and sub-assemblies and could not plan ahead, but plenty of practice had made him an expert in crisis management and he expected to shine when all about him was going haywire. McTaggart on the other hand was jealous of his boss getting such a big order while his efforts, such as they were, were more modest.

To some extent McTaggart's prophesies of disaster had some justification. By heroic efforts and much cajoling of his staff, Bill Batty got the Spanish orders done in time, but only just. Moreover, that was at the expense of the smaller orders that McTaggart brought in from his inadequate forays into the UK market. His customers complained and McTaggart was more disgruntled than ever. He got George to give him a young man to stay in the office and do the telephone sales, but it was noticeable that McTaggart still seemed to spend a deal of time at headquarters. It was at this time that a kind of alliance was formed between McTaggart and Batty to blame anything that went wrong on poor George.

One of the good features of the Spanish deals was that very prompt payment was specified and the Spaniards fulfilled their obligations. This was a very welcome boost to the cash flow, and for a while the bank exercised a less clumsy pressure. But George had now got the bit between his teeth. His young designer was making improvements that helped to sell more, and George spent more and more time away from his desk doing what he enjoyed most and at which he was personally most successful.

When George and his accountant went over the quarterly results the accountant pleaded for drastic reorganization. The firm was grossly overtrading both financially and organizationally. Bill Batty had many virtues as a production engineer, he knew what should be done and how to get the best out his workers, but the paper work and planning side were utterly beyond him. George must spend more time in the works. As for McTaggart, if he could not be made to perform he should be replaced by someone who would.

Genial George was very averse to any kind of quarrel or altercation, and was more than a little afraid of McTaggart's aggressive nature. He went and consulted the local Enterprise Agency. His adviser was clear that his present management structure was completely inadequate. After lengthy discussion it was agreed that:

- George should stay in the office as much as possible, and assist and control Bill Batty in the workshop and that he should take a closer interest in all that went on. As the adviser said, 'There is no better management tool than the boss's eye.'
- McTaggart should be chased out of the office to do the job he was paid for.
- An experienced procurement manager should be employed to support Batty and control the quality assurance person.
- There should be a management meeting late on every Friday afternoon to review the week's problems and make decisions for the future. It was hoped that, if everyone had had some say, a spirit of cooperation would prevail. This meeting would be attended by George (in the chair); his wife, Millicent; the book-

keeper, Bill Batty; the procurement expert, McTaggart (allowed back into the office for this occasion only); and an adviser from the Enterprise Agency.

■ There should be a formal board meeting every month with George, Millicent, the two directors and the firm's accountant and auditor.

It was hoped that this new management plan would overcome the problems that had plagued the firm since it started. The product was good; the market was there. Everything depended on good management. Time would tell.

7

The market

That the size and availability of the market is of major importance to the budding entrepreneur was emphasized in Chapter 1. However good your product or service and however well managed your business, you will never achieve success unless:

- you have a market of adequate size;
- you have identified your customers;
- you know what they really want;
- you know how to reach them.

The marketing history of one Bruce Entwistle can be used to illustrate the above points.

Bruce had invented a simple little kitchen gadget. Having made a prototype, he carried out some basic market research into its acceptability to the end user. What he did was to ask as many housewives as he could contact whether they would be prepared to buy one and how much they would pay. Having satisfied himself that the product would sell, he considered the next step.

The housewives of the United Kingdom obviously could not be his direct customers. He could not make a living by going from door to door with his inexpensive little gadget. The costs of tooling up for production meant that he would have to sell the gadget in tens of thousands to make any profit.

Selling large quantities of any line costs a lot of money, however it is done. Bruce was going to be hard pushed to cover the tooling-up costs for production, so he had to reject ideas such as employing a team of door-to-door salespeople or starting a mail order campaign. He had to reject, too, the idea of selling through individual retail shops. The shopkeepers could not be his direct customers either, as it would be far too expensive to set up the necessary organization and employ sales representatives. Eventually he decided to approach the buyers of one or two chain stores. They were interested. They told him what modifications they wanted made to his design and what terms of sale and delivery they required. He negotiated sufficient orders to set up his business and go into production.

Bruce Entwistle had fulfilled the criteria set out above:

- he had satisfied himself that there was an adequate market among the housewives of the United Kingdom;
- he had identified his customers as the buyers of kitchen items for the big retailing multiples;
- he had made his product and terms acceptable to those customers;
- he had found a path of distribution to his end users.

Let us consider how the people in our examples tackled the market.

The situation of Alexander Battersby (Example 3.1, page 31) was relatively simple. He knew there was a market in Ourtown for joinery. His uncle George had been earning a living as a joiner for many years, and Alexander was taking over his business. Alexander knew there was competition but trusted in his skill to meet it. One can criticize him on two counts: first, because he did not make himself aware of his customers' feelings (see Chapter 12), and, second, because his efforts to sell his services were not sufficiently positive, relying too much on word of mouth and a rather vague advertising policy.

Rosemary Rambler and Muriel Tonks (Example 5.2, page 74) had done their homework on the market before they made their decision to start. They selected the sort of customers they thought would buy their product and went out and met some of them. They not only confirmed that the market was there; they also got some firm orders. One would not expect marketing to be their major problem. Indeed, their market was a very wide one and apt for the use of the internet. As we shall see, when these two dipped their toes into this market the results were spectacular.

Nicola Grant (Example 3.2, page 41) had her market defined for her. It consisted of the customers coming into Mr and Mrs Smith's grocery shop. Her problem resolved itself into deciding whether this market, or even a practicable extension of it, would be large enough to pay her overheads and yield a sufficient profit. Nicola decided it would not. If Nicola had been intending to open a new shop rather than buy an existing one, she would have had to involve herself in much more elaborate procedures: finding out how many shops were selling her type of goods in the area, how many possible customers passed the door of the premises she had in mind and so on.

Robert Herrick and Deirdre Williams (Example 4.2, page 55), buying Lamplights Electrical Store, were acquiring a ready-made market; but at the same time they were going to invest a lot of money in expanding one aspect of the existing business. Robert was already in the trade and knew the local scene well, but he still went to the trouble of visiting 30 out of 49 of his potential customers. He was able to make an estimate of the total trade available to him. His contacts convinced him that he would be able to obtain a sufficient proportion of that trade.

The market research of the inventor Marcus Garside (Example 5.1, page 72), was necessarily more perfunctory. He knew there was a need for an improved seat-belt reel, but he had to take a chance that there would be a market for his particular product when he had designed it and that there would be a customer for his patent.

The makers of the left-handed snooker cues (Example 5.3, page 85) carried out a more elaborate market research programme than any other described in this book. James Turbotte did his desk research on the number of left-handed persons. He then set in train a formal quantitative market canvass to find the number of potential users of left-handed cues. Finally, he researched his method of distribution and decided to use Galligaskin and Breeks.

The examples of J S Brook (Example 6.1, page 96) and Bradfield Techtonics (Example 6.2, page 101), the expanding businesses, have half their problem solved in that, since they have been successful so far, we can assume that the market is adequate. However, the reader of a business plan must be convinced that the available market is large enough to sustain the expanded business and that it is not moving either to saturation or towards a new fashion.

J S Brook (Example 6.1) has two supports for his belief in the Wagbatch Marina. He knows that in the previous year the demand was greater than the supply because he had to turn away potential customers, and he knows that the number of boats needing berths is going up at present by 5 per cent each year. (According to the best estimates available, the limit of canal capacity will not be reached for a few years.)

As far as marketing is concerned, Bradfield Tectonics Ltd (Example 6.2) is in a very special position. The need for expansion and finance has arisen from a sudden increase in demand for the product. The company will still have need of an active marketing policy, but a shortage of sales is not likely to be the chief problem in the foreseeable future.

George Weston's company (Example 6.3, page 106) is what we can call 'market led'. George is a born market man and selling will not be his problem. Indeed, his problems will arise because of his skill and preoccupations with selling his product.

All the people in our examples, except possibly Marcus, the inventor, had to be sure that there was a market. They knew that unless they had enough customers there would be no profit for them. They did not proceed on pure hope or a simple faith in the value of their product or service; nor did they place much reliance on the encouragement of their friends. The examples show the means they employed to find out, as best they could, whether an adequate market did, or did not, exist.

No one has ever gone bust through over-estimating the laziness of his or her customers. I am not saying that most of your customers are lazy or procrastinators. Many are conscientious, industrious people; but they will not be upset if you make things as easy as possible. However, you may quite well lose the business of lazy people for the most trifling reason. Remember that it is not your job to punish them for being lazy, and remember too that their money is just as good as anyone else's – if you can get it.

For instance, if you are dealing with the public or small businesses they are unlikely to be sitting in a well equipped and organized office. The chore of answering a letter of yours or of sending back an order form is often more than lazy people will do briskly or promptly. You will make it easier for them and more likely that they will give you the order if you send them a pre-addressed envelope or, if you think it is worthwhile, a stamped preaddressed envelope.

Make your order forms simple and easy to fill in. Indeed, if you are canvassing an individual you know already, you could try filling in some of the information before you send it (taking care to get your facts right, such as the name and address of the individual). Above all, avoid jargon.

Make sure your full address and postcode are on all types of correspondence. Don't make the customer have to hunt around for your address, especially if it is a long one. This brings us to the question of your telephone. Despite the development of modern electronic means of communication, the 19th-century invention of Alexander Graham Bell is still the public's favourite method of communication, especially for queries and complaints. Large companies find the telephone an expensive form of communication, and the very size of their organization turns their telephone network into a cat's cradle of complexity. Far too often this cat's cradle is used by the lower levels of a bureaucracy to bamboozle, delay and complicate a difficult query in the hope that the customer will go away and stop being a nuisance.

Small businesses are, or should be, immune to this problem. One or at most three well-trained receptionists will solve the issue. They will know who will deal with each type of query and where such members of the firm are. Indeed, they may be quite capable of dealing with some simple inquiries by themselves and will become familiar with many clients. An intelligent receptionist, who knows his or her way around your business, is discreet and with a gentle voice, can do your firm immense good and should be treated generously.

But the very small business, such as a joiner, an electrician and the like, cannot afford a specialist receptionist. I hold that all small business owners should carry a good mobile phone with them and keep it always switched on so as to be able to answer it, however busy they are.

May I suggest that your receptionist could well use any time he or she has left in ringing up clients on a list prepared by yourself to see whether and how your work satisfied them, and to ask whether they have any queries. Such assiduity can only do good: 'my supplier cares about me' is a feeling much to be encouraged.

Example 7.1: Norbury Williams

As said above, no one has ever gone bust because he or she over-estimated the laziness of customers or clients, though many do so by under-estimating it. However, catering for the lethargy and procrastination of human beings has brought fortunes to many. I am going to give an account of one who got a flying start by making the most of this factor. Unlike my other stories, this is not in any way imaginary but is a true statement of something that really happened. Only the name and place have been changed – everything else is true.

Norbury Williams was a skilled mechanic with garden machinery. He quarrelled with his uncle who employed him and decided to try his luck on his own. Eventually he visited the local enterprise agency. His adviser there was already harassed by the difficulty of taking his own lawnmower to the repair shop in the boot of his car. He suggested that as Norbury had a low-loading trailer he should offer to go round and pick up the lawnmowers, thereby relieving his customers of the awkward chore of loading up their own machines into a car boot. He could even charge a bit more for offering this extra service.

The adviser suggested that Norbury have some cards printed with his new way of doing business and push them through the letterboxes of potential customers. The adviser suggested the area to canvass should be Rollsley, a well-known prosperous suburb where folk would be less likely to begrudge the higher price. Norbury, a bit of a psychologist, said Friday evening was the best time to take the cards round, as on Saturday morning the man of the house would already have lawn mowing and lawnmowers lurking in his mind. This was agreed, and Norbury said he would come back on Monday and report any progress.

But he didn't. Nothing was heard of him all week. But the following Monday he came in to apologize, saying that he had been so busy carting lawnmowers around and dealing with them that he had had no time left. He had even been stopped by the police, who wanted to know what he was doing with a truck full of lawnmowers. Norbury explained. 'Right,' said the police officer 'and when you have dealt with those, you can come and pick up mine.'

8

Planning the borrowing

Many firms go under through bad planning of their finances. It would be tragic if, with all your management skills, and with a large market for a fine product or service, you were to fail at the last because of money problems.

There are businesses that have come into being and have flourished without any money being raised except for the proprietor's own. Sturdily independent, even in the raising of finance, the owners have sacrificed rapid growth for the security that owing nothing to anyone brings. However, this chapter will assume that either you cannot 'go it alone' as regards the money, or that you believe your opportunity should be exploited more rapidly than self-financing could possibly achieve. So you have decided to take the risk of borrowing.

Now you must decide what is the most efficient way of borrowing and how much you can risk. Again, your best guide when making your decision is the cash flow forecast you are preparing as an essential part of your business plan.

Take the simplest of our examples first. Alexander Battersby (Example 3.1, page 31) needs money to get started, but his cash flow forecast shows him that he will not need it for long, and he intends always to be in the black at the bank thereafter, barring accidents. His customers pay him in cash, so once he has paid off his starting loan, that should be that. Alexander needs only a simple over-draft facility. To take out a term loan would be inappropriate, as Alexander would go on paying interest on the balance even when his current account was in the black – which would be nice for the bank, but not so good for Battersby & Co.

Other entrepreneurs' situations are quite different. When Alexander did a job, he got paid for it right away. He even managed to buy half his materials on credit, so the more jobs he got, the faster the money rolled into his bank account. Not so for, say, Turbotte Manufacturing Ltd (the makers of the cues, Example 5.3, page 85). For every contract they undertook, they had to pay out wages to their workers for days, or even weeks, before they could send out an invoice; and even then there was a delay before they were paid. The money they needed to lay out on producing the goods before getting paid is termed 'working capital'.

Most businesses have to borrow over a longer period, and they have to be sure that the money is available as required. They do not want to have to make repeated calls on the bank. They will try to negotiate a term loan with as long a 'holiday' as possible before any repayment of principal need be made.

In Example 5.2 (page 74), Rosemary and Muriel were in an intermediate position. They gave the same period of credit to their customers that they obtained from their major suppliers. The only delay in their cash flow will fall between receipt of the invoices for metal and casting and the date on which they can invoice their statues outwards. Their profit margin is good, so sales generate working capital. On the other hand, their overheads are quite heavy, and they are spending money on publicity and on designing and making new moulds.

Rosemary and Muriel's policy must be, therefore, to fight for more production, so that they can sell more statues. Their borrowing reflects this, in that they took out a term loan with a nine-month moratorium on repayment of the principal. This allows them the necessary time before profits exceed overheads and new design costs, etc. They also arranged for an overdraft facility to cover any delays in achieving a really positive cash flow. As events showed, this was wise. The Stanislavski delays threw a strain on their cash position, but their solution of the production problem has put them back into credit.

In Example 3.2 (page 41), Nicola's business planning persuaded her to give up the idea of buying the Smiths' food shop. But let us consider the buyer of a truly profitable retail shop obtained at an economic price.

The essential basis of good retailing is that you buy from your suppliers on credit and sell to your customers for cash (or for cash through a banker's credit card system). Thus your cash flow is likely to be strongly positive, and the more you trade the faster the bank balance builds up – so long as you control your buying.

There are two siren voices in a retailer's ear, one saying, 'If you buy in larger quantities you will get a bigger discount,' and the other, 'If you extend your range you will reap more sales.' Both assertions are true as far as they go, but both are fraught with danger. Acting on the first puts in jeopardy the retailer's advantage of buying on credit and selling for cash. Indeed, if you buy for more than two months' sales, the cash flow becomes negative because you have had money 'out' to suppliers for longer than you have had it 'in' from customers.

Acting on the second and increasing your range will not be truly profitable unless the increase in sales is at least proportionate to the increase in the cost of your stock. The ideal policy is to aim for rapid turnover of a limited range of goods.

If you keep your buying under proper control, a retail shop should need no increase in working capital once you have started trading. You ought not to find it difficult to pay for an increase in stock out of increasing profits. Indeed, in your first months your cash flow should be distinctly positive, as you are selling for cash, while your first payments for new goods will not be made until the second month. Allow for this in deciding how much you want to borrow on a term loan and how much on an overdraft.

Because the capital involved in buying a shop – stock, fixtures and goodwill – is usually high in relation to the profits to be earned, you will try to negotiate terms to repay the loan over several years; but since your ongoing working capital requirements should be nil, you ought to be able to start repaying almost at once.

If, in addition to buying the business, you are buying the property and can raise the money to do so, my advice is to look upon the two purchases as separate propositions. The one is a venture in retail trade, the other a speculation in shop property. One could prove worthwhile and the other not, depending on circumstances. A separate financing of the property on a long-term basis should be your aim.

When it comes to the Wagbatch Marina (Example 6.1, page 96), the means employed to raise the finance for its extension are even simpler and more straightforward. John S Brook has borrowed money to build up an income-generating asset. As long as he can let his berths, the money will roll in, steadily increasing the cash flow. He will arrange a term loan, to be paid off in instalments, these to begin as soon as the berths are ready for letting.

In the examples discussed so far in this chapter, the financing problems were fairly cut and dried. The obvious resource was some form of bank loan which could be covered by collateral. (When you borrow money, you are under a personal obligation to pay it back. The bank will require a guarantee, however, beyond your personal word. This *collateral* could take the form of a second mortgage on your house, the assignment of an insurance policy, or a signed undertaking by a property owner prepared to repay the loan should you be unable to do so.) What remained to be discussed, though important, was simply the willingness of the bank to lend, the form of the loan and the rate of repayment.

If your fund-raising problem is similar to one of those discussed above, then go to several banks to get the best terms offered. Two rules apply. First, take along a copy of your cash flow forecast when you go to negotiate repayment terms, and second, take care not to agree to earlier repayments than you will be able to make without difficulty.

Incidentally, if you are thinking of taking out a mortgage on your house to raise finance, it is worth considering an approach to your building society. It may be able to give you a better deal than the bank is prepared to offer. Always remember that your house is at risk if you use it as collateral.

The projects introduced as Examples 4.2 (Herrick and Williams, page 55), 5.3 (Turbotte, Fletcher and Watchman, page 85) and 6.2 (Allen and Spooner, page 101) are larger and the financing more complex. None of the companies could offer sufficient collateral to cover the amount of money needed, even if it were appropriate to obtain the entire sum as a loan from the bank.

Anyone making such a loan to one of these companies would be running a risk, as the company might very well fail. Companies do fail, all too frequently. The lenders of unsecured money have to cover their losses on the failures out of the profits they make on the winners. This pushes the interest rate on a straight, unsecured loan up to the 30 per cent mark for all but the most thoroughly researched and copper-bottomed propositions. No responsible bank or similar institution would want to lend to Ourtown Electrical Supplies, Turbotte Manufacturing Ltd or Bradfield Tectonics at 30 per cent. The interest rate itself would cripple almost any business. In fact, many businesses are pushed into liquidation by the horrific cash flow burdens placed on them by high rates of interest and harsh loan repayment terms.

The government, aware of the problem, has instituted the Small Firms Loan Guarantee Scheme (SFLGS). Under this, the government itself acts as guarantor to the bank for the majority of the money the bank lends, and the loan can be made without requiring personal security. There are two snags. First, because there is no security, the rate of interest is higher, and second, since the bank is still lending some of the loan without security, it scrutinizes SFLGS propositions much more closely than it does requests for ordinary secured loans.

Your best course, if you want to avoid these high interest rates, is to find a source of 'equity' capital. What does the term 'equity' mean? Originally, of course, it referred to even-handed dealing. Next it was used by lawyers to mean a system of justice which supplemented the rules of the common law of the old traditional courts. By derivation it has come to mean, in financial contexts, actual ownership of part of a company, as distinct from merely lending money to it. An ordinary shareholder actually owns part of the company. If 10,000 shares in a company are issued and you own 100 of these, you own 1 per cent of the company. Ordinary shares are therefore 'equity' shares.

In general, all ordinary shares are of equal value and have equal rights; but it is legally possible to have ordinary shares which have lesser rights, say as regards voting, as long as they are issued on that understanding. However, both the Stock Exchange and some government departments dislike such distinctions and discrimination.

There are some shares that have a mixed or disguised nature. The wit of financial experts has invented all sorts of 'mixed' investments, either to meet special needs or to help with tax problems. Preference shares are really loan stock pretending to be shares. They come in several flavours. They are 'participating' preference shares, which are a kind of half-breed. They have a fixed interest element, like a loan, plus a little share in the profits, like ordinary shares. They are said to have some 'equity element'. Some preference shares or loan stock are given the title 'convertible'. This usually means that they can, according to the rules laid down at their birth, undergo a sex-change, as it were, and become equity in the form of ordinary shares. These non-standard shares are tricky and are best avoided by most small companies. If your company wants to consider issuing such shares, it is essential that you seek expert advice.

But issuing ordinary shares to sell part of the equity is common enough, though there are people who object strongly to 'selling part of my company'. Some even see it as 'giving it away'. If this attitude is based on an overwhelming desire for independence at all costs, that is a personal view and no one can quarrel with it. But if it is grounded in a determination to make as much money as possible and keep the lot, that is greedy – and foolish as well. There is a good deal to be said for selling equity – provided you can get satisfactory terms.

The person, company or bank lending you money is entitled to interest and the return of the money in the proper time. This is true – come profit, come loss, come positive cash flow, come negative cash flow. Inconvenient or even ruinous to you though it may be, lenders must get their money. Not so your equity shareholders, who are with you through thick and thin, in good times and in bad. Your equity shareholders can get money only when you do, and in proportion to their shareholding. Good equity shareholders are an excellent source of finance. Treat them well. Psychologically they are taking a greater risk than you are. You are in control of the joint enterprise. Remember how much more jittery you are in the passenger seat of a car than when you are doing the driving. So don't begrudge equity shareholders their share of the profits.

But where are these providers of equity capital to be found? Most prudent people are very cautious of buying minority shareholdings. They know only too well that whoever owns 50.1 per cent of a company's shares effectively controls it as far as day-to-day running is concerned; and anyone holding more than 75 per cent can even alter the company's rule book, the Articles of Association.

When you are looking for people to invest in your business, only family, friends and existing business associates who trust you are likely to put their money your way. Unless, that is, you go to a first-class commercial lawyer who can devise a scheme for giving your minority shareholders protection.

'But where,' you may ask, 'are these venture capital companies we hear so much about?' Venture capital companies do exist, and some of them deserve the name. Whole books have been written about venture capital, and it is not possible in one chapter of a book on business plans to do more than offer one or two general comments.

Such companies can be divided up, variously, as follows:

- those that will invest in new start-ups;
- those that will not;
- those that will help, indeed insist on helping, in management;
- those that have a 'hands-off' approach;
- those that genuinely offer 'risk' money;
- those that are purely money lenders.

What virtually all of them have in common, however, is an inability to help the business which needs anything less than £150,000.

There are two very good reasons for this. The first is the cost of investigating your proposition. The venture capital company does not know you from Adam. It is unlikely to know much, of itself, about the sort of business you are proposing. All it knows is that you have written a good business plan. So now experts have to be paid to check out your proposal. Their investigation may cost £7,500 or more. On an investment of £150,000 over five years, that £7,500 represents only 1 per cent per annum. But on a loan of merely £20,000, it comes to 5 per cent per annum. There is a further point to be taken into consideration: that these costs are incurred even if the venture capital company should decide against advancing the money. The successful loans have to cover such costs too. It is easy to see why these companies are not willing to lend sums of less than £150,000.

The second reason is that a small start-up company is deemed unlikely to have sufficient all-round management skills. The only venture capital company likely to be interested is one that has a definite 'hands-on' approach and will expect to have a say in the management. This is not necessarily a bad deal for a new company, but the costs are too great to make an investment of less than £150,000 by the venture capital company worthwhile.

It is apparent that a big funding gap exists below the investment level of £150,000 and above the level at which it is possible to obtain secured bank loans on reasonable repayment terms. This gap is an acknowledged one, not least by some government agencies, and discussions are under way with the aim of finding solutions to the problem. Some local initiatives are in operation. Your local Business Link will be able to tell you whether an organization of this kind is to be found in your area.

Such equity funding as is available often comes with offers of, or insistence upon, management support in one field or another. This is not to be spurned or despised. Few companies have no weaknesses in their management portfolio of skills, and if such an offer is made, it should be given serious consideration. It is not recommended that you be indiscriminate in accepting such offers of assistance. Some are far from disinterested, and at best, agreeing to take on a partner is like accepting a marriage proposal. You have to be sure that you will get on, not only when it is warm and the moon is shining over a calm tropical sea, but on a cold, wet Monday morning in Witherspool, when the bills are coming in through the letter box.

Let us consider how our three remaining companies (Examples 4.2, 5.3 and 6.2) tackled the problem of raising finance.

The directors of Ourtown Electrical Supplies Ltd (Example 4.2, page 55) came up with an ingenious ploy. Making use of the government's Enterprise Investment Scheme (EIS), they approached potential customers and invited them to invest in their enterprise. Under the terms of this scheme, the well-to-do and fairly well-to-do could invest in a small company and have the amount of their investment deducted from their gross income for tax assessment. It appealed, naturally, to the higher tax-rated. They had to keep this money in for five years, and there were other conditions and restrictions. It was cheap compared with venture capital investment and had no cash flow disadvantage until the five years were up. In the case of Ourtown Electrical Supplies Ltd, the investors knew the extent of the market, and indeed were themselves a substantial part of it. Their belief in the company's success had a self-fulfilling element. Good luck to them!

Turbotte Manufacturing Ltd (Example 5.3, page 85) took the Guaranteed Loan Scheme line and obtained the money needed. The loan was a little more expensive than the directors would have liked, and it must be repaid in due course. If the company's long-term plans work out, in a few years Turbotte will be coming back for a second tier of finance, probably from 3i, a venture capital fund or a merchant bank.

The Bradfield Tectonics Company (Example 6.2, page 101) is large enough to be able to approach a venture capital company or a merchant bank. It will choose carefully what organization to approach. Some venture capital firms have special interests, and one with a 'high-tech' bias is more likely to be willing to invest. There are others that are really only interested in quick capital gains. They can bring pressure on a successful company to be taken over or to go on to the Alternative Investment Market (AIM). Dr Allen and his colleagues may not want this and should avoid such firms.

This chapter is not intended to be a comprehensive account of the ways in which an individual or firm can raise money, but is an attempt to show how your method of financing your business must be related to its size, its nature and your plans for its future. When you talk to your financial advisers now, I hope it will be with a clearer idea of what you require and how to go about getting it.

9

How not to write a business plan – or run a business

A business plan, to succeed in its aim of raising money, must persuade the reader that four main aspects have been properly covered. It must show:

- that a sufficient market exists;
- that the management will be capable and efficient;
- that the product or service is good;
- that the finance will be adequate to meet requirements and reasonable contingencies.

Your business plan should demonstrate all-round strength and competence. Exhibiting brilliance in one or two aspects is not enough. The Duke of Wellington, to cite an example from history, has never been rated a 'brilliant' general. He was, however, extremely successful, never lost a battle and lived to an honoured old age. When asked for the secret of his success, he said he never neglected any detail, however small, that might contribute to victory.

The Iron Duke's principle can be applied equally well to running a business. The duke knew that training, feeding and supplying his troops and paying due attention to the other aspects of running any army were at least as important as the tactics employed in battle. He could perhaps be better described as a successful managing director of his army than as a military genius.

Following the duke's maxim, your business plan should cover not only the exciting aspects of the business, but the humdrum and tedious ones as well. It is not necessary to set out in detail who will send out statements or make the tea or make sure that the corridors are clean; but the reader of the business plan must be made to feel that somebody will be responsible for dealing efficiently with these matters.

Two business plans I have read illustrate how people can get carried away and allow an individual aspect to dominate their thinking to the exclusion of almost everything else. Both these plans had been written by people of superior education, but neither would have persuaded any worldly-wise financier to invest his or her money. While both men were full of fire and enthusiasm for their separate projects, neither gave space to the more mundane problems of management and administration, so that the resulting plans were hopelessly unbalanced. Below the weaknesses of both these plans are described in some detail, but in such a way, of course, that neither can be identified.

The first example came straight out of one of our major universities. The author was clearly fascinated by the technological breakthrough that he believed his colleagues had made. He wrote pages about the advances in solid state physics that had made the project feasible. He very carefully referenced his claims from the scientific point of view, but it was not until he came to page 4 that mention was made of ways in which this technical or scientific break-through might be applied in any commercial sense. And even then, commercial application seemed to slip in as a side issue, and this despite the fact that the author was hoping to receive considerable sums of money for development and research.

The next few pages were devoted to describing some interesting ideas the technologists had in mind, but there was no indication as to how the research and development, when completed, could be turned into a profit-making enter-prise. A formal cash flow was given at the end of the document, but this seemed little more than a ritual exercise. The figures used had no apparent derivation from anything in the rest of the 'plan'.

This might almost be given as a classic case of enthusiasm for a technological advance running far, far ahead of the commercial considerations involved. To summarize the mistakes made in this business plan:

- Far too much technical information was given, little of which would be comprehensible to the reader.
- No clear line of development was given, nor was a profit forecast. The days have long gone when boards of directors and others were prepared to shell out large sums of money on the say-so of technologists who were 'baffling them with science'.
- The applicants did not start by describing the market for their product, so there was nothing to excite the interest of the money people unless and until they first waded through pages of physics.

- The names of the distinguished scientists who had done the research were mentioned, but there was no indication as to who would be running the enterprise, nor any hint that a management structure had been thought about.

There was no plan of action at all, save to do some more developmental research. Some technological innovation, doubtless excellent of its kind, an awareness of a large potential market for at least one product, and a plea for more funds do not constitute even the beginning of the sort of business plan likely to attract commercial finance. Perhaps, with a major shift in emphasis from the technology to the potential product itself and its market, and with an improvement in clarity, this document could have been used to sell the idea to an existing firm for, say, a payment in royalties. But as a plan designed to show how a company would operate and make use of the money being sought, it was utterly useless.

The second example of an upmarket, blundering business plan is more commercially sophisticated. However, it does share one grievous fault with the first example. This case involved biological technology in which quite a few people have at least a grounding in the basic science. And yet, while reading the first few paragraphs, anyone might have wondered what the author was talking about. It could be gathered that there was a market for some kind of product, but so many newly minted terms had been used that it took a real effort to translate the text into comprehensible English.

Excessive use of technical terms or jargon is a disease not only of high science and technology. All professions, sports or trades – be they butcher, baker or candlestick-maker – use or develop words with special meanings. Sometimes these words constitute a useful form of shorthand for a new idea; but too many are mere variants, intended to impress or baffle the outsider. Such technical terms or jargon phrases should not be used in a business plan, at least not without some explanation of their meaning. You are not trying to dumb-found your reader, but to show him or her your clear grasp of the situation.

Let us return to our second bad example – the biotechnological enterprise. The faults here were not limited to an over-indulgence in jargon when writing the formal plan. They ran deeper. The plan displayed a fundamental imbalance in the way the company and its problems were perceived. Originally formed to supply goods to a market thirsting for the products, the company had been on the verge of foundering owing to failures of manufacture, in both quality and quantity. It was rescued through the skill and reorganization effected by a first-class production engineer from another discipline. Now, or so the writers of the business plan appeared to believe, a further injection of capital was all that was needed to ensure the company's future prosperity. The market was taken for granted. At the moment the company could sell all it produced, and it was assumed that this happy state of affairs would continue indefinitely. There was in the plan no indication that the company had a marketing policy or that the writers of the plan foresaw the need for one. Nor was there evidence that they had set up a well-thought-out management structure or any system of financial controls.

You cannot take for granted such matters as who is going to be responsible for what and how the money will be controlled, let alone that a marketing policy will not be needed in the foreseeable future. No one should ever invest money in any concern until satisfied that these aspects have been given adequate consideration and a proper plan has been made to deal with them.

'But,' you may well ask, 'what lessons are there in these two examples for the very small business?' It is true that in both these cases sums of about £250,000 were sought; but the very same problems face the individual about to start on his or her own with, at the most, part-time help. Indeed, the problem shown in the first example confronts almost every sole entrepreneur who wants to manufacture and sell a product, whatever it may be.

The people who wrote the first plan were not clear what kind of business they wanted to be in. Are you? Let us say that you have decided there is a future in the handcuff business. Now where is your strength? Are you a designer of handcuffs? Or a skilled craftsperson or production engineer? Do you, perhaps through a working life spent with Interpol, know the world market for handcuffs and who the buyers are? Or are you a good manager, with financial and administrative skills, who has seen an opportunity in the handcuff trade? Unless you have pots of money and an already established market, you cannot afford to buy in all the management skills you need to supplement your own – that is, if you want to control the whole process, from design to selling the finished product. So choose your line. Either make handcuffs and let someone else sell them; or sell handcuffs and contract out the manufacture to someone else.

Take, for example, a small manufacturing concern making a first-class, moderately priced engineering product, well thought-of in the trade, and with potential for vastly greater sales. It is a very small business: the owner, with some part-time help, does everything himself. And there is his problem. He designed the product, he makes it himself at the bench, he does the selling and the paperwork and writes up the books. He attends business management courses and seminars. He works very hard, and yet the business grows at a snail's pace. In 15 or 20 years, if his health holds and his product is not superseded, he may achieve a reasonable income and no longer have to work 70 hours a week for 50 weeks of the year. As things are, he just cannot bring himself to let go of any part of the business and thus reduce his workload and the number of problems he has to solve.

It is true that there have been individuals who won fame by building up big businesses from almost nothing. But such people are becoming increasingly rare as business life grows more complicated. Those who succeed in this way must have flair amounting to genius. This book is not aimed at business geniuses; it is intended for those of us with more modest abilities who hope to make the most of what resources we have.

If you have read the business plans of the snooker-cue makers and of the two ladies in the garden statuary business, you will have noticed that in neither case do they intend to run everything, from designing to selling, themselves. The statues are going to be fabricated by someone else, and the snooker cues, for the time being, are going to be sold by another firm. The financiers to whom the plans are presented will see that in both cases energy and resources are going to be concentrated where it matters most, and that in consequence, the number of day-to-day problems with which the managers will have to grapple will be much reduced.

It is sometimes said that there are just not enough experienced people with management skills to go round. In the United States, the financial houses judge business plans more by the management ability offered than by any other factor, certainly more than by the excellence of the product itself; and they insist that the management must be 'balanced'.

By balanced, they mean that the various aspects of management should not outweigh one another. A business may sometimes be referred to as 'market-led', or alternatively 'design-led'. These are jargon terms for a real, though rather vague, concept. What 'market-led' should not mean, however, is that sales managers make all the decisions and grab every order they can lay their hands on, while those in charge of production and finance have to struggle desperately, and all too often hopelessly, to catch up.

'Design-led' should not mean that talented designers or design engineers can insist on all their wonderful ideas being put into production despite the protests of the marketing side or the horror expressed by the finance director. Every side of management, whether represented by a separate person or in the compartments of the mind of a sole proprietor, should be able to admonish with a 'Hey, slow up there', or encourage with a 'Come on, get moving', and do so effectively. This is what balanced management is about. Build this balanced management into your plan, and make it clear to the reader of your plan that the balance is there.

The question of balance in management is crucial. That does not mean simply paying proper attention to the design side, to selling and to production.

These are the interesting aspects for which everyone sees the need. But the boring side of business is equally vital to success: sound bookkeeping, good stores control, etc – in short, all those jobs you did not go into business on your own to do. We all know about firms who go bust despite having a fine product and expert salespeople, but whose office and stores administration can only be described as slovenly. They often write up the books days or even weeks late. They rarely deliver spares in the time promised, fail to answer queries, delay sending out invoices and – before they have grasped what is happening – suddenly find themselves in the hands of the receiver.

To revert to the Iron Duke's maxim, Napoleonic plans of tremendous breadth and vision are fine, but Wellington's attention to detail won the battle of Waterloo.

10

Maintaining the plan

So! You have started. You have produced a fine plan, and persuaded your banker to lend you the money you need. This plan is kept handy – not put away in a bottom drawer. You intend to re-read it regularly to make sure you are still on course. But will you be able to tell in good time whether you are still on course?

You will get a rough idea as you go along. You have orders coming in and so far the bank has not been on the phone about the overdraft. On the other hand, that overdraft is worrying, and one supplier has been chasing you about the bill. You sometimes wake up in the night afraid that fate may be waiting with a sockful of sand to hit you on the head. You wish you could find the time to look into the problem.

Very wisely, you decided you could not afford the fancy management accounting systems that a computer salesperson on a fat commission tried to sell you. What you do not need is a mass of documents to have to read through and understand – trading accounts, profit and loss accounts, balance sheets, bank reconciliation statements, cash flow analyses, etc. It would take at least an hour of careful, professional study to understand them. No! What you do need is a simple statement of your current position and the actual trends of your business. These trends are important, and it is these trends that you have to watch. There are three figures you will need to note every day:

- your balance at the bank;
- the amount of money owed to you (by your 'debtors');
- the amount of money you owe (to your 'creditors').

Comparing these figures daily with yesterday's figures and those of a week ago, and a month ago, six months ago and a year ago, can tell you a great deal about how your business is progressing. Analysing them will help you to plan for further success on a firm basis or, if the signs are less rosy, to take remedial action.

How can you obtain these figures daily without using a computer? It is easy enough, if you make it a rigid rule that all financial transactions are entered in the books on the day they occur. All cash and cheques received, and all payments, must be entered every day. A record must be kept of all invoices sent out during the day, and of all invoices and other bills received. Much as you may hate bookkeeping, this is essential, as putting it off, even if only until the end of the week, just makes for more work and worry in the end. With the figures in front of you, you can do little sums that take just a minute or two. These can be very revealing – see Table 10.1.

Table 10.1   Working out daily figures

Enter yesterday's cash balance	£232.19
Add cheques and cash received today	54.50
	£286.69
Deduct cheques and cash paid out today	
To suppliers	£100.00
Other expenses	£53.99
	£153.99
Today's cash balance is, therefore	**£132.70**
Enter yesterday's amount due from debtors	£2,017.70
Add invoices sent out	150.00
	£2,167.70
Deduct cash and cheques received today	54.50
Today's debtor balance is therefore	**£2,113.20**
Enter yesterday's amounts due to be paid	£983.67
Add invoices received	125.00
	£1,108.67
Deduct amounts paid out	100.00
Today's creditor balance is therefore	**£1,008.67**

If, as you go along, you enter these calculations in some sort of loose-leaf book, it is simple to add the corresponding figures for the same day last week, the same date last month, and if you wish, for three months, six months and nine months; and of course (if available) those of the same date last year. You are now building up a whole library of information about your business, which is all the more valuable because it is bang up to date!

A very useful form of 'internal audit' is to compare these calculated figures for debtors and creditors with the lists of actual monies owed to you and monies owed by you to suppliers. This should eliminate mistakes. You will be able to keep abreast day by day and brood over these figures while you are driving or in the dark watches of the night.

Let us take as an example Sammy Brooks, who makes circuit boards for various firms in the electronics industry. He has adopted a system like the one outlined above, and watches the trends in his business carefully. He has been busier than ever over the past few months, and his sales have been growing. This shows up in his daily financial reports. There is a steady rise in the value of what his debtors owe him. A smaller but significant rise has been showing up in the amount he owes his creditors, and more worryingly, there has been a gradual increase in the bank overdraft.

Sammy ponders all this. The overdraft is nowhere near its limit, but the trend is all the wrong way, and he certainly does not want to be in the position of annoying his suppliers by not being able to pay them on time. He knows that he has neither drawn out any more money than usual for his personal use, nor spent money on useless stock or new equipment. He even turned down the salesperson's request for a new computer, tempted though he was by the gadgetry. He wondered whether his profit margin was too low, but no, his prices were if anything on the top side, as his quality was high. Sammy decided to consult his accountant/adviser and talk it over with him.

Between them they decided that the business was doing more work than it could cope with. Sammy said the factory could turn out even more circuit boards: he had the equipment and he had the workers. The accountant said that this was not the point. Every time a new job was taken on, the business had to meet costs for materials and continue to pay wages. This money would be going out long before customers sent in their cheques. The more rapidly Sammy's business expanded, the sharper would be the pressure on the bank account.

Sammy suggested going to the bank to ask for a bigger overdraft facility, but the accountant was dubious. Banks, he declared, were very unwilling to finance this sort of 'over-trading' (as it was called). He could offer a different solution, provided Sammy was prepared to let the orders slack off a little. 'Turn the difficulty into an opportunity,' he suggested. The business could well stand an increase in prices, if what Sammy told him was true. He could put up his prices a little and look for customers who were prepared to pay more for a first-class product, while at the same time he could offer them a slightly increased discount for cash. If a customer failed to take the discount, Sammy would make more profit on the contract, and when someone took the discount, the money would come in all the sooner.

Even if sales fell off a little, the business would just be 'cooling off' a bit, and Sammy would get more profit and cash flow in relation to the effort he was putting in. With the financial control system he had adopted, it would be easy to find out whether the change in tactics was working out. Moreover, if the overdraft was reducing and the debtor balance falling, it would be a sure indication that the order book could be expanded again.

Let us now take the case of Reginald Mowbray. Reginald had not been trained for any occupation, but he was a genial fellow and had friends all over the place. One day, when he was at a loose end, one of these friends spoke of a wine-growing area in the south of France that was about to start a big publicity campaign extolling a new range of local wines. Reginald saw his opportunity. 'If I can get some supplies, I can get in on this,' he said to himself. By using his network of friends, he found a supplier, and through contacts with owners and managers of clubs and restaurants, he was able to build up a good list of customers for these new wines. So far he was proving himself a successful entrepreneur.

Despite his purely literary education, Reginald understood business. He realized that as the wines became better known, big companies would move in, and eventually he would be squeezed out. He needed to know when the pressure was likely to grow too great. On the one hand, he did not want to quit before he was hurt; on the other, he felt he must not carry on too long and find himself left with heavy commitments to his suppliers and a lot of stock he could sell only at a loss.

So he adopted a daily record system like the one advocated above. Thus he was able to keep on a straight path while on the 'up and up'. But in time he noticed that supplies were harder to come by at the old prices. Moreover, his daily system showed that the amount of money owed to him was starting to go down, and soon a fall in the amount of money he owed followed. His bank balance was showing a steady increase, and he had more money to spend.

The writing was on the wall. It was a warning that the easy days were coming to an end. What should he do? With his experience in the field and his success record, he was able, through his friends, to find a job as a wine buyer for one of the firms moving in on the business. At the same time, he was able to turn into cash all his investment in stock and come out with a nice profit in ready money.

Both Sammy and Reginald could have gone badly wrong, had they not had a solid day-to-day knowledge of what was going on. A business genius may possess some sixth sense, but most of us do not. We need prompting. We need early warning systems. Something like what I have suggested above is essential to increase the odds in favour of success.

But there are aspects of planning, other than the purely financial, that require constant appraisal. Surely one of the most valuable of your assets in the business is your own time. Are you spending that time wisely? I am not asking whether you are giving enough of it to the business, for I am sure that you are. You are almost certainly working more hours than when you were an employee, and you should not begrudge yourself your leisure time, your amusements and your hobby, for they will keep you sane. No, I am talking about the time you actually spend on the business. Is that properly planned and controlled?

Look back at the story of George Weston in Chapter 6. Setting aside George's temperament, was he concentrating on his function as chief executive of the company in which all his money was invested? No, he was not. His mind was too often away on the next sales pitch, and he did not like to have to deal with the production problems of the touchy assembly-shop manager, or having to goad the reluctant McTaggart out on his rounds. Moreover, he was not interested in the books and reluctant to talk about the overdraft.

The management re-planning was constructed to make sure of a balanced management, as talked of in Chapter 9. One of its purposes was to keep George in the office and the ambitious but lazy McTaggart out of it. George should now be able to exercise that most effective of management tools – the boss's eye. There is an old saying, 'organization is delegation', but delegation is usually fruitless without 'supervision'. Hence the need for a proper management plan and for its maintenance.

Another failure in management can come about through over-concentration on an otherwise excellent precept. One of the first things you learn in life is that what you know is far less important than who you know. Paddling your own canoe is hard work indeed if you have no friends and acquaintances to help you on your way. So it is important that any up and coming entrepreneur should get around and do some networking. This is one of the reasons that business people become masons or Rotarians, join expensive golf clubs when they do not like golf particularly, or take part in local politics. All this is good stuff for increasing the influence of your business, and it is indeed the duty of the head of a business to maintain this influence.

I remember many, many years ago a client firm in East Lancashire, realizing that power was ebbing away from Manchester to London, together with what once were local banks and procurement agencies, decided that their sales director, on the verge of retirement, should go and open an office in London. As he said to me, his real work now was to play golf on the right courses in Surrey with the right people – and let them just beat him on the 18th so that he could 'spin' away on the 19th, with a glass in his hand and the person he wished to influence in the right mood. His colleagues back in Lancashire could then attend to their business without distraction.

All this is good as far as your own business is concerned; it's the right stuff for increasing the influence of your own business, and it is indeed the prime duty of the head of a business to perform it. But there is danger. You can spend too much time, which you should use in supervising your colleagues, in visits to and lunches with people outside whom you think may be useful contacts. As I have said – keep it balanced.

Another way in which chief executives can jeopardize their companies by misusing their time is, to put it bluntly, by minding other people's business for them. Now do not get me wrong. God knows we need men and women in public life who have had years of experience of competent business management. From the House of Commons, through quangos, management boards and coordinating committees of all kinds down to primary school governorships, there is a desperate need for more men and women who have proved they can get things done, and done promptly and properly.

But need it be you? Can your business spare you at this stage in your career? The first claim on your energy and time is your business, including its employees, customers and suppliers. High authority has it that no man can serve two masters – he will cleave to the one and despise the other. When the business is no longer your boss and when you are effectively semi-retired, then you are in a position to attend to public welfare. In the mean time remember the principle of balance.

This is what I suggest for you: a daily time sheet in which you record how you spent your time. Many firms, very rightly, have such time sheets for even their senior staff. Why should you demand order and method in the way your staff spend time, while your even more valuable time is left to whim and chance? If you keep some kind of record of how you have used your own time, you can make regular checks to see that you are giving balanced attention to all that is going on and not simply concentrating on what you do best and what is most interesting. It is so often those aspects of your business that bore you most that will produce the blocks on which you may stumble.

Preparing business plans is an ongoing activity, not just a start-up operation to be put aside and forgotten. If the above emphasis on daily bookkeeping and on recording your own time seems too tiresome and pettifogging, it is because you have not yet appreciated the importance of overall control. They will help you to run your business and not let your business run you. Before you get into trouble is the time to learn control, not when the bank and your creditors are sitting on your neck.

11

Small business and the trade cycle

Everyone has heard of trade cycles occurring in waves of alternate boom and slump, but not all business people are aware that they should take such cycles into account when formulating their plans and activities. These booms and slumps have been with us since time immemorial. Certainly, they occurred in the Middle Ages, and one book suggests that successive phases in the building of Stonehenge followed the pattern of a Bronze Age trade cycle. Theories abound as to why we have these ups and downs, with little or no level ground between them. But the authorities cannot agree, though politicians like to blame the government of the day whenever a slump occurs.

Leaving theories to one side, the fact remains that in the Great Depression of 1929–33, when the 'capitalist' United States had millions of unemployed, in 'socialist' Russia millions more were dying of starvation or being shipped off to slave labour camps. It is unfortunate that politicians, especially those in charge of a country's finance, should claim they have solved trade cycle problems. Such boasting, to score a point at political opponents, is deplorable. No one should believe a claim that 'we have abolished the old boom and bust of the other party'. There is no evidence of this, and readers of this book should still take all the necessary precautions.

If governments or professional economists are unable to control a slump or depression, what hope, you may ask, can there be for you and your small business? Admittedly, it is tragic for those whose businesses fail; but it is nevertheless true that the majority of established businesses do manage to survive. How, then, can you ensure that your business will be one of the surviving majority?

You can make a good start by developing an awareness of trade cycles and determining at what stage of the cycle you find yourself. It is often easier to recognize when a slump is over than when a boom is going sour. This is probably because both politicians and financial journalists would rather make optimistic statements than forecast doom and gloom. But there are signs to guide you; for example, trends on the Stock Exchange, variations in taxation revenues and house prices, which are discussed in the financial columns of newspapers.

Clearly, it is risky to start a new business, or to borrow money to expand an established one, at the top of a boom. For one thing, your sales are going to be harder to come by as the downturn develops, and to make things worse, your costs will continue to rise until the slump makes itself well and truly felt. Remember how wages and salaries continued to spiral upwards in 1989 and 1990, although it was obvious that the downturn would soon be on its way. Worse still, if you have heavy borrowings, the inevitable increase in interest rates makes the debt burden heavier, and as a final turn of the screw, your customers, themselves the victims of the downturn, pay you later and later, and you have to borrow yet more money just to keep your business afloat.

On the other hand, if you can get a business started or keep an existing one going in the depths of a depression, the future is much rosier. If there is still a market for your product or service, your sales will become easier. At the same time, your costs will rise more slowly than your sales, the interest on your loans will fall, and your customers will find it easier to pay you.

Let us suppose that you are starting a new business at the bottom of a depression, or planning the future strategy of one that has survived. You decide that, on the basis of past history, the trade cycle covers a period of probably 10 years – five years to the top of the boom, followed by five years to the bottom of the next depression.

In Chapter 1 you were advised to include in the business plan that you will put before your bank manager a paragraph devoted to the 'longer-term view'. This is intended to cover the years of expansion. But it is worth having a private strategy to cover those years when you may not only be no longer expanding but may actually have to retrench.

At this point it is worth remembering that some businesses are more affected by the trade cycle than others. Dispensing chemists and funeral directors are inherently stable, but builders, metal fabricators and sellers of luxury goods (such as cameras or bone china) are far more dependent on prosperous times and find themselves bearing the brunt of the depression when it comes. If yours is an average business, subject to the usual cycle of boom and slump, you could expect:

- 2.5 years of very hard work;
- 2.5 years of good profitable expansion;

- 2.5 years of good profits, even though the boom is past its peak;
- 2.5 years of real downturn.

In an ideal world you would have, or could borrow, enough money to acquire, by the end of two and a half years, all the fixed assets needed for the cycle, have paid off all the loans after five years and have accumulated enough cash in the next two and a half years to enable you to snap up the bargains that will be on offer in the next recession.

But we do not live in an ideal world. Although logically and statistically it is less risky to launch a business with a good marketable product at the bottom of a slump, you will find the necessary capital hard to come by. So you may have to wait until a little later in the cycle. If so, remember that you will have fewer years in which to expand. Also, of course, your product or service may be a late starter in the trade cycle or even have a shorter life as a profit-maker because of changes in fashion.

None the less, the principle remains: prepare for the lean years. When the economy starts to turn downhill, cash is king. So some guidelines can be laid down:

- All money to buy plant and machinery and goodwill should be paid off by the middle of the trade cycle.
- Money still owed by the business at that time should be significantly less than the floating assets (ie debtors, stock and cash).
- The business should have, by then, a strong positive cash flow.

There may be good reasons for buying plant during the downturn or borrowing money for expansion, but this is an ultra-long-term strategy and is more appropriate to a large company. A small business person is well advised not to swim against the tide.

Can the principle of preparedness apply to other factors in your business? Yes, it can. (We are assuming that you have now adopted the strategy of paying off debts while the going is good and ensuring that you have cash on hand as times falter.) Take, first, your responsibility to your employees. One of the most painful duties an employer can face is having to sack someone, and laying off a good employee in a downturn is extremely distressing. How can you plan so as to avoid or minimize the necessity for laying off staff?

Bear in mind that the higher the proportion of your wage bill for piecework, bonus payments or overtime, the more your takings can be allowed to fall before you have to sack anyone. Most people would rather have no overtime than no job. Consider, too, the possibility of employing older people, who may be retiring in any case by the time the downturn is due. You may feel uncomfortable at the thought of taking on people who are considerably older than yourself, but remember how valuable an experienced and conscientious older person can be.

If redundancies have to be made so that the business can survive – and a business cannot survive if it is not profitable – the sooner they are made, the better. This may sound hard-hearted, but, remember, those released are more likely to find new jobs if the 'sacking' is done before the recession has deepened. What is more, by releasing some staff early, you are more likely to be able to retain your remaining employees. You have a responsibility to them too.

Think before taking on unnecessary financial commitments. The art of running a business includes the ability to distinguish between what is necessary and what is merely desirable. Money is hard to earn and expensive to borrow. You will need working capital and 'the tools of the trade' (which may mean plant and machinery), but do you have to buy premises? Consider carefully: you may be doubling the stakes for a relatively small return.

In Chapter 8 it was recommended that running the shop and owning the property should be regarded as two separate enterprises. Whatever your business, becoming a property owner means taking on an additional commitment. Can you afford the risk of borrowing for two enterprises?

It follows, too, that you should be wary of expanding your lifestyle while you are in debt over the business. Remember, if you have personally guaranteed any loan to your 'limited' company, you have, in effect, borrowed the money yourself. If you are borrowing money for your business, you cannot afford a larger house, a bigger car, an expensive holiday and so on until your debt is reducing, until the business is really profitable and generating cash. Even if your cash flow and your profit and loss forecasts show a surplus after a few months, this does not mean that the predictions are bound to come true. In nine cases out of 10 you will have been over-optimistic, particularly about the rate at which sales will increase. Be patient and don't count your chickens before they are hatched.

Many a business has failed not because of inherent weakness or even increasingly high interest rates, but because it could not support its own borrowings and the owner's increased personal debts. Avoid what is called the 'Jaguar syndrome'. This afflicts many a small business owner. Things are no more affordable just because you can buy them 'through the business'. So, unless it is absolutely necessary for the business, do not buy that additional computer or trendy office furniture until you are making and cashing profits; and don't replace the old family saloon with an impressive 'executive' car until the profits are substantial.

You may also suffer in a recession through the difficulties or failure of one or more customers, even though your own business is free from any inherent weakness. At any time, a slow payer is a bad customer and should be treated accordingly; in hard times, he or she is even more of a nuisance, and is the one most likely to saddle you with a bad debt.

It may be that, by the very nature of your business, you have just a few customers, perhaps only one. This puts you at a greatly increased risk during a recession: if one customer fails to pay, you could face ruin. In your planned strategy, therefore, not only must you have a tight system for control over your debtors and for monitoring the continuing creditworthiness of your customers. You should also consider carefully whether the extra costs involved in dealing with many smaller customers are not outweighed by the high risk of having only one or two big ones. Big contracts entail big risks.

In general, to avoid the worst features of the trade cycle and ride out a recession, remember the old Boy Scout motto: be prepared.

12

Monitoring progress

In this chapter it is assumed that you have obtained your money from the bank, have started up and are now well into your stride. Perhaps you are doing better than you expected, or perhaps worse. Do you really know how you are doing? You will know if you have followed the advice in Chapter 2 and used your cash flow forecast as a budgetary control. Do you remember what the suggestion was? You were to fill in the 'actual' columns with the figures you actually achieved, thereby keeping abreast of what was happening. You should also have kept a copy, not only of the formal business plan you sent to the bank, but also of the more detailed plan you drew up initially. Constant re-reading of this document keeps you in touch with your original plan.

One of the dangers for the person running a small business is preoccupation with the day-to-day problems. The more work on hand, the truer this is. From the self-employed service trader, working around the clock on a seasonal flush of jobs, to the owner of a factory, struggling to complete a big order, the story is the same: there is no time to think until the latest crisis has been overcome. The danger is that in solving each problem as it arises, or indeed, in grabbing at an opportunity as it occurs, you can be diverted from your true path almost without realizing it.

If you have a partner or a trusted manager, you should be talking to him or her regularly about the business. You should review your plan at regular intervals – even if you do it alone. Get out your business plan and your latest updated cash flow forecast, then go over all aspects of the business in the light of the figures, so that what needs changing, what needs slowing down, what needs speeding up, and where to go next can be considered and resolved.

It is very useful to have an interested and friendly outsider present at this meeting. The obvious person is your accountant. The good, modern accountant is no longer content just to prepare accounts at the year end – or some months after – and agree your tax bill with the Inspector. He or she should be eager to give regular help and advice. If you are lucky enough to have a competent, up-to-date accountant, make use of the services on offer. The fees per hour may sound very high, but the advice may well prove invaluable.

You may decide to call at your local Enterprise Agency to discuss your plans and your hopes and fears. The counsellors there will be delighted to see you, and the service is free. A regular visit at three-monthly intervals is recommended, so that your progress can be monitored. If the staff cannot come up with an answer to your every question, at least you will be told where you can go for specialist help. And, in any case, just talking about it can often clarify a problem and bring a solution to mind.

There are two other groups of people who have an interest in your success: your main suppliers and your chief customers, with individuals in both groups who, if they themselves are good at what they do, will be pleased to help you become more efficient and prosperous. Visit them regularly. They will prove to be a major source of information, tips and advice. Try to call on them just before you hold your 'mini' directors' meetings, so that their views can be considered too.

In the following pages you will be able to find out how the various characters whose business plans were described earlier progressed and developed their ideas. The interesting ones are those starting up in business for the first time. The others can be assumed to be able to look after themselves.

As might be expected, each of the start-up examples runs into one typical sort of problem or another, and you will see how their difficulties are overcome.

Example 3.1: Alexander Battersby (page 31)

Alexander Battersby, the skilled joiner, did keep track of how his business was progressing. His job in doing so was made relatively easy because Doreen Gray was looking after his books. Keeping the books bang up to date is the necessary basis of good management, whether the business is a corner shop or a multinational.

You can see on the bank forecast form in Table 12.1 how it worked out for the first six months. The outgoings have been fairly accurately

Table 12.1   Alexander Battersby's cash flow forecast

Cash flow forecast for: A Battersby   Month January to June

	Jan		Feb		Mar		Apr		May		June		Totals	
Receipts	Budget	Actual	Budget	Actual	Budget	Actual	Budget	Actual	Budget	Actual	Budget	Actual	Budget	Actual
Cash sales	750	740	950	957	1150	1018	1150	1251	1200	1138	1200	1251	6400	6355
Cash from debtors														
Capital introduced	1800	1800											1800	1800
Total receipts (a)	2550	2540	950	957	1150	1018	1150	1251	1200	1138	1200	1251	8200	8155
Payments														
Payments to creditors			45	44	57	57	69	61	69	75	72	68	312	305
Cash purchases	45	44	57	57	69	61	69	75	72	68	72	75	384	380
Rent/rates/water	60	60	60	60	60	60	60	60	60	60	60	60	360	360
Insurance	300	300											300	300
Repairs/renewals	20	12	20	8	20	25	20	10	20	20	20	5	120	80
Heat/light/power					50	60			50			45	100	105
Advertising	100	115				30				35	50		150	180
Printing/stationery			5	11	5	4	5	8	5	8	5	3	25	34
Transport/motor expenses	60	65	60	67	260	281	60	71	60	63	260	255	760	802
Telephone					50	50					50	50	100	100
Professional fees (D Gray)			100	100	100	100	100	100	100	100	100	100	500	500
Capital payments	1500	1500											1500	1500
Interest charges							35	38					35	38
Drawings	500	500	500	500	500	500	500	500	500	500	500	500	3000	3000
Licences and sundries	150	150											150	150
Total payments (b)	2735	2746	847	847	1171	1228	918	923	936	929	1189	1161	7796	7834
New cash flow (a–b)	-185	-206	103	110	-21	-210	232	328	264	209	11	90		
Opening bank balance	Nil	Nil	-185	-206	-82	-96	-103	-306	129	22	393	231		
Closing bank balance	-185	-206	-82	-96	-103	-306	129	22	393	231	404	321		

NB: All figures include VAT

forecast. The motor expenses are a little higher than expected, but Alexander has not had to use any money for contingencies – yet.

On the other hand, Alexander had noticed pretty early on that he was not getting enough work by word of mouth recommendation. He got the expected work from builders, and the DIY rescue work was, if anything, better than forecast, thanks to his friend at the DIY shop; but the private house work was not up to expectation. Although it was Alexander's long-term plan to develop the subcontracting side of his business, he could not help worrying about this shortfall in the work on private homes. He knew the jobs he had done were first class, and yet the householders did not seem to be recommending him to their friends and neighbours.

After three months in the business, Alexander decided to call at the local Business Link. The counsellor listened to what he had to say, discussed with him ideas for advertising and publicity, then put a few rather searching questions to Alexander:

- Were there occasions when he did not turn up at the time agreed?
- Did he ever fail to let the householder know when he could not keep an appointment?
- Did he sometimes neglect to tidy up after finishing a job?
- Had he left doors open when going in and out of the house?
- Did he smoke without first asking permission
- Did he keep his radio going full blast?

Despite feeling somewhat resentful at being asked such questions, Alexander had to admit that he had been guilty on most of these counts. On one occasion he had not finished the morning's job by lunchtime and did not let his next customer know because 'it was a bit awkward to phone'. The lady was furious, as she had taken an afternoon off work to see the job done. There was another time when something similar had happened. He denied that he had ever left without sweeping up; he took too much pride in his work to allow that. But he did admit that he was a bad one for leaving doors open – a customer was always complaining – and he was a heavy smoker.

The counsellor emphasized that Alexander was in what is called a service industry, and success would depend not just on doing a fine job technically but also on pleasing the customers in every way, even if some of them seemed to him unnecessarily fussy.

When the counsellor had a look at the cash flow forecast, he said that if everything went as planned, Alexander would have tax to pay. Fairly big payments might fall due in 18 months or two years' time, which could come as a very nasty surprise if money was not put by in readiness. He suggested that 20 per cent of the turnover in excess of £650 per month should be put into a building society account. Not only would this enable Alexander to pay the tax when it came due, but also the savings would be earning interest in the meantime.

As a result of this interview, Alexander mended his ways, and towards the end of six months, found he was getting a good number of jobs through private recommendations. In fact, as the bank forecast shows, his sales in June were better than expected.

Example 5.2: Rosemary Rambler and Muriel Tonks (page 74)

During the first six months Rosemary and Muriel found themselves in danger of being blown off course owing to the Stanislavski Foundry falling behind with its own capacity expansion programme. Not only was production for months 3, 4 and 5 going to be affected, but also the planned production for the whole of the year was put at risk.

Muriel drew up a new cash flow schedule for the year. For the first three months she entered what actually had happened; for the next nine the figures were based on the new production forecasts of the foundry, with savings on advertising costs, as it would be no use advertising goods they would not have on hand to sell. The result, as shown in Table 12.2, was not encouraging.

Action was taken immediately. Rosemary and Muriel went to see the managing director of Stanislavski. The meeting was a little stormy. The MD promised to do what he could, but he talked too much about his own difficulties and the cheap price Rosemary and Muriel were paying. Rosemary then went to call at another foundry in the Bristol area. Here she was given the red carpet treatment, and a contract was signed for four statues a month, production to begin at once, with a promise of four more per month in six months' time.

The new moulds, including the one for the rampant lion (which was proving especially popular), were sent to Bristol. As soon as the MD of Stanislavski heard of this, he called on Rosemary. He had good news, he said. He had managed to overcome his difficulties, and by the end of the month after next would be able to increase production to five statues per month. In four months' time the foundry would be able to turn out 10 statues per month, and there would be no increase in price.

As the orders had been rolling in, Rosemary and Muriel knew they could sell all they could produce. Their cash flow forecast had to be brought up to date yet again. This time they would include further costs for design and moulds, as there was a strong demand for a wider range of models and it was obvious they would need some paid help.

At the end of six months the cash flow forecasts were amended once more, this time to show the actual results for the first half year and the improved prospects for the second half. These new forecasts are shown in Table 12.3.

Now Rosemary and Muriel reviewed their business plan in the light of their latest forecasts and the very healthy demand for their statues. They had their accountant from Belt & Braces in on the discussion. It was decided they should:

- carry on with the same marketing and advertising procedures;
- design a large range of statues (one hotel firm wrote, 'People don't want to see a Copenhagen Mermaid in every foyer throughout England');
- follow up a marketing idea of Muriel's: to make smaller statues for private houses and gardens;

Table 12.2 Muriel's new cash flow schedule

Rosemary Rambler and Muriel Tonks
First revised profit and loss and cash flow forecasts
After three months' trading

Profit and loss account

	Month 1	Month 2	Month 3	Month 4	Month 5	Month 6	Month 7	Month 8	Month 9	Month 10	Month 11	Month 12	Total
Number of statues sold	1	2	2	3	3	3	3	3	3	4	4	4	35
Value of sales	650	1,300	1,300	1,950	1,950	1,950	1,950	1,950	1,950	2,600	2,600	2,600	22,750
less													
Metal and casting	285	570	570	855	855	855	855	855	855	1,140	1,140	1,140	9,975
Moulds and design	20	40	40	60	60	60	60	60	60	80	80	80	700
Overheads	962	962	962	962	962	962	962	962	962	962	962	962	11,544
Interest	47	47	47	47	47	47	47	47	47	41	41	41	546
Wages													0
Depreciation	67	67	67	67	67	67	67	67	67	67	67	67	804
Profit	-731	-386	-386	-41	-41	-41	-41	-41	-41	310	310	310	-819

Cash flow forecast

	Month 1	Month 2	Month 3	Month 4	Month 5	Month 6	Month 7	Month 8	Month 9	Month 10	Month 11	Month 12	Total
Receipts from sales		764	1,528	1,528	2,291	2,291	2,291	2,291	2,291	2,291	3,055	3,055	23,676
Loans	4,000												4,000
Other receipts	4,000												4,000
Total receipts	8,000	764	1,528	1,528	2,291	2,291	2,291	2,291	2,291	2,291	3,055	3,055	31,676
Payments for:													
Metal and casting	0	670	670	1,005	1,005	1,005	1,005	1,005	1,005	1,340	1,340	1,340	11,390
Moulding materials	453	340	0	57	230	230	57	57	230	230	57	57	1,998
Ditto wages	65	65				60				60			250
Overheads	2,192	788	878	1,046	529	644	1,796	529	644	1,046	489	604	11,185
Interest			141			141			141			123	546
Other wages													0
Drawings	500	500	500	500	500	500	500	500	500	500	500	500	6,000
Capital payments	3,600												3,600
VAT				-705			45			81			-579
Loan repayments									500			500	1,000
Total payments	6,810	2,363	2,189	1,903	2,264	2,580	3,403	2,091	3,020	3,257	2,386	3,124	35,390
Balance	1,190	-1,599	-661	-375	27	-289	-1,112	200	-729	-966	669	-69	-3,714
Bank balance	1,190	-409	-1,070	-1,445	-1,418	-1,707	-2,819	-2,619	-3,348	-4,314	-3,645	-3,714	

Table 12.3 Amended cash flow forecast for Rosemary and Muriel

Rosemary Rambler and Muriel Tonks
Second revised profit and loss and cash flow forecasts
After negotiating new production contracts

Profit and loss account

	Month 1	Month 2	Month 3	Month 4	Month 5	Month 6	Month 7	Month 8	Month 9	Month 10	Month 11	Month 12	Total
Number of statues sold	1	2	2	3	7	9	9	9	10	12	14	14	92
Value of sales	650	1,300	1,300	1,950	4,550	5,850	5,850	5,850	6,500	7,800	9,100	9,100	59,800
less													
Metal and casting	285	570	570	855	1,995	2,565	2,565	2,565	2,850	3,420	3,990	3,990	26,220
Moulds and design	20	40	40	60	140	180	180	180	200	240	280	280	1,840
Overheads	962	962	962	962	962	962	962	962	962	962	962	962	11,544
Interest	47	47	47	47	47	47	47	47	47	41	41	41	546
Wages									200	200	200	200	800
Depreciation	67	67	67	67	67	67	67	67	67	67	67	67	804
Profit	−731	−386	−386	−41	1,339	2,029	2,029	2,029	2,174	2,870	3,560	3,560	18,046

Cash flow forecast

	Month 1	Month 2	Month 3	Month 4	Month 5	Month 6	Month 7	Month 8	Month 9	Month 10	Month 11	Month 12	Total
Receipts from sales		764	1,528	1,528	2,291	5,346	6,874	6,874	6,874	7,638	9,165	10,693	59,573
Loans	4,000												4,000
Other receipts	4,000												4,000
Total receipts	8,000	764	1,528	1,528	2,291	5,346	6,874	6,874	6,874	7,638	9,165	10,693	67,573
Payments for:													
Metal and casting	0	670	670	1,005	2,344	3,014	3,014	3,014	3,349	4,019	4,688	4,688	30,474
Moulding materials	453	340	0	230	230	230	230	230	230	230	230	230	2,863
Ditto wages	65	65				60	250	250	250	250	250	250	1,690
Overheads	2,192	788	878	1,046	529	644	1,796	529	644	1,046	489	604	11,185
Interest			141			141			141			123	546
Other wages									200	200	200	200	800
Drawings	500	500	500	500	500	500	500	500	500	500	500	500	6,000
Capital payments	3,600												3,600
VAT				-705			68			1,015			378
Loan repayments									500			500	1,000
Total payments	6,810	2,363	2,189	2,076	3,603	4,589	5,858	4,523	5,814	7,260	6,357	7,095	58,536
Balance	1,190	-1,599	-661	-548	-1,312	757	1,016	2,351	1,060	378	2,808	3,597	9,037
Bank balance	1,190	-409	-1,070	-1,618	-2,930	-2,173	-1,157	1,194	2,254	2,632	5,440	9,037	

■ employ a full-time assistant, preferably an art college graduate, to enable them to increase production;

■ seek out yet another foundry, to both keep their two existing suppliers on their toes and provide for further expansion.

The accountant congratulated them on the progress they had made, saying they would soon have a business of which they could be proud.

The accountant also suggested to them that their product was an ideal one to sell worldwide on the internet. Muriel took up this idea with enthusiasm, and had an expert in to set up their own website. The results were startling. Within the first week they had two enquiries from Poland for statues of Winston Churchill. It looks as if the future is bright for these two women.

Example 3.2: Nicola Grant (page 41)

As you will remember, Nicola's business planning had persuaded her not to start at all. She was glad of this when, some months later, it became obvious that Mr and Mrs Smith's grocery business was going downhill. However, the exercise of working out the figures and making up her mind to give up a lovely dream had convinced Nicola that she was not as stupid and feeble as she had been made to feel at times in the past. Before her marriage Nicola had worked in an office, and she decided to take a course at the local College of Adult Education to learn word processing and the use of information technology in general. Nicola has a part-time job now, working in an office in Witherspool, and is feeling much more pleased with herself.

Example 4.2: Robert Herrick and Deirdre Williams (page 55)

A loan was successfully negotiated with a local bank under the Loan Guarantee Scheme (LGS). Unfortunately, there were unforeseen delays over the lease. The solicitors, Redd, Herring and Co for the company and Manyana, Manyana & Holliday for the lessors, were unable to complete the formalities, despite extensive and protracted correspondence, until well into the new year.

This delay produced a series of damaging consequences:

- The company was two months late in launching its comprehensive service to the electrical trade. This gave the competitors from Bradfield an opportunity to ginger up their own services and forestall Ourtown Electrical Supplies Ltd. One firm went so far as to open a branch in Witherspool.
- Two of the working electricians, who had planned to put up some of the capital under the EIS scheme, got fed up and backed out. To make up the shortfall, Mr Lamplight agreed to a delay in the payment to him of a part (£4,000) of the sum he was to receive for his stock.
- The company found itself landed with a large range of fancy electrical gift items which had been ordered for Christmas. (It had been possible to cancel only one or two orders without penalty.) The cash flow position was so bad by the time the Verges Street premises opened that the business had to be started with a 'Sale'.
- The publicized gala opening took place at a dead time of year. Bobby Lovebird was no longer able to attend; and the whole affair fell rather flat.
- The legal arrangements were much more complicated than had been expected, and the legal costs were almost twice what had been budgeted for. Unfortunately, by the terms of the lease, Ourtown Electrical Supplies Ltd had to bear the whole of these costs.

Table 12.4 Ourtown Electrical Supplies new profit forecast and cash flow forecast

Ourtown Electrical Supplies Ltd
Financial projections for first year's trading
as amended after six months' trading

Profit and loss account

	Month 2	Month 3	Month 4	Month 5	Month 6	Month 7	Month 8	Month 9	Month 10	Month 11	Month 12	Month 1	Total
Sales	11,858	16,455	19,509	21,867	25,492	28,202	28,100	29,600	22,200	34,000	37,000	37,000	311,283
less													
Cost of goods sold	8,398	12,576	14,085	15,834	18,597	20,614	20,518	21,680	16,260	24,775	27,100	27,100	227,537
Overheads	6,373	6,373	6,373	6,373	6,373	6,373	6,373	6,373	6,373	6,373	6,373	6,373	76,476
Interest on overdraft			105	30	75	75	90	75	63	60	30		603
Interest on loan	333	315	298	280	263	245	228	210	193	175	158	140	2,838
Depreciation	313	677	677	677	677	677	677	677	677	677	677	677	7,760
Net profit	−3,559	−3,486	−2,029	−1,327	−493	218	214	585	−1,366	1,940	2,662	2,710	−3,931

Table 12.4 *continued*

Cash flow forecast

	Month 2	Month 3	Month 4	Month 5	Month 6	Month 7	Month 8	Month 9	Month 10	Month 11	Month 12	Month 1	Total
Sales payments	3,483	13,193	19,421	23,077	26,342	30,111	32,630	33,476	32,342	30,856	38,752	42,947	
Loans	30,000												
Capital introduced	50,000												
Total receipts	83,483	13,193	19,421	23,077	26,342	30,111	32,630	33,476	33,342	30,856	38,752	42,947	
Purchase payments	2,045	19,876	14,954	16,756	18,930	22,089	24,210	24,245	24,837	20,106	29,384	31,843	
Overhead payments	11,504	9,323	6,612	5,906	4,197	4,887	5,756	6,760	4,887	5,656	6,455	4,582	
Interest			1,048			968			858			563	
Loan repayments	1,500	1,500	1,500	1,500	1,500	1,500	1,500	1,500	1,500	1,500	1,500	1,500	
Capital items	17,625		20,563				4,700						
Opening stock (inc VAT)	15,275												
VAT				-6,243			2,963			2,769			
Total payments	47,949	30,699	44,677	17,919	24,627	29,444	39,129	32,505	32,082	30,031	37,339	38,488	
Cash flow	35,535	-17,506	-25,255	5,158	1,716	667	-6,499	971	260	824	1,412	4,459	
Bank													
Opening balance	0	35,535	18,028	-7,227	-2,069	-353	313	-6,185	-5,214	-4,954	-4,130	-2,717	
Closing balance	35,535	18,028	-7,227	-2,069	-353	313	-6,185	-5,214	-4,954	-4,130	-2,717	1,742	

The long-term effects of the delayed opening – through opportunities given to competitors, disappointment suffered by important customers, etc – are hard to assess; but even in the short term the effect on cash flow could have been disastrous if the company had not budgeted for more in the way of financial resources than a strict analysis of requirements demanded.

As it was, the company survived – just. The local electrical contractors remained loyal, and the company has proved itself able to offer a first-class and economical service. The new showroom is beginning to be visited by the public, and this gives hope for retail trade in the future.

Although six months have not yet gone by since the nearly disastrous start, the books show that sales are not far off the original monthly target, and in fact are growing at a slightly better rate than forecast. Everyone still has hopes of a bright future for the company, though things may never be quite as good as if the delay had not occurred.

The accountants drew up a new profit forecast and cash flow to the end of the year, including the actual results for the first five months (Table 12.4). They assumed that the company would be back on monthly sales targets by the end of the year. But the delay over the lease, which could not have happened at a worse time of the year, had a dreadful effect on both profit and bank balance, as you can see.

The moral is that once you are committed to a plan, any delay in getting properly started can be very expensive. In this case it was a legal delay, but it could have been a building contractor's delay, the failure of a financial sponsor to come up with the money on time, non-delivery of machinery or any of a number of other things. I know of an enterprise in which £250,000 had been invested. Because some computer software had not been fully tested and was not running properly until a fortnight after the business was launched, the whole enterprise collapsed and all participants lost their money.

Do not rely on promises of delivery. Allow for some inevitable delays. But do not tell your contractors you are doing so! Otherwise they will take their period of grace and still be late. Have them on a savage penalty clause for delay – if you can.

Example 4.3: Osbert Wilkinson (page 65)

For three months Osbert's restaurant was a really great success. His tables were filled almost every evening. His average number of customers per night was 42 rather than the 32 that he had counted on; his chef and partner, Guy Loosely, was turning out delectable meals and varying them sensibly, and his staff did not neglect the customers. They did not even keep them hanging around waiting for the bill. Moreover, he was able to get a bigger average payment per head than that for which he had once budgeted. Perhaps fancifully, he attributed this to his choice of music. He had read an article in the trade press in which a psychologist had suggested that 'up-market' music induced a desire for 'up-market' food. Osbert, a music lover himself, now believes that Mozart increases his average bill by a significant amount!

Osbert even got a good price for his lunchtime trade because he targeted the local business people and provided lunches that impressed their clients. For weeks the lunchroom was pleasantly full. Then a blow fell. Osbert's place was some distance from the centre of town, too far for people to walk comfortably. In the evening there was sufficient parking around but at lunchtime the kerbs were all full or double yellow-lined. He thought he had solved the problem by an agreement that his customers could use a strip of land nearby owned by a developer. This worked until one morning the empty site was full of contractor's material. The owner had sold the site without telling Osbert. His good lunchtime trade just collapsed, except for Saturdays and Sundays when there was enough kerb space unoccupied.

Osbert revised his plan. His special lunchtime staff had to go, as the weekend lunch trade could now be covered by a rota of his regular staff and stand-by part-timers. His variable overheads for lunchtimes were reduced from £40,000 (see page 68) to £12,000, but the proportional contribution of trade at lunchtime to his fixed overheads (see page 67) was much reduced. This was undoubtedly unfortunate, as the total profit he enjoyed at first was reduced by the loss of five days' lunchtime trade, but Osbert is still doing very well and can feel pleased with himself.

The congestion due to shortage of parking space is becoming a very real handicap to many kinds of small business. The sudden imposition of double yellow lines has often proved the *coup de grace* for many a small shopkeeper who has no opportunity or resources to move out to a greenfield site complete with its own parking places. You are well advised to consider how parking congestion will affect you now or in the future; this does not apply only to the retail traders.

Example 5.1: Marcus Garside (page 72)

Marcus was very pleased with the way in which production of his prototypes went forward. What is more, the testing showed that his seat-belt design was far superior to anything else in its class on the market. However, now he began to run into difficulties. He had assumed that once he had developed his design and patented it, he would be able to find an agent or broker to help him sell his rights; but no such person or firm could be found. His patent agent said that he could not actually help to sell the patent for reasons of professional ethics; and neither his accountant nor his solicitor knew of any source of help. Two non-profit-making organizations were generous with advice, but for actually doing the job of selling his patent Marcus was on his own. Truly, as stated at the beginning of Chapter 5, the path of an inventor is hard – especially in the United Kingdom.

Bewildered but determined, Marcus set about finding a firm to take on his product. Naturally, he tried the local ones first; then others in the United Kingdom. All turned him down, giving one reason or another. A marketing organization, however, was impressed by the product, and one of its directors suggested a deal: if Marcus formed his own company to manufacture the seat belt, the marketing people would do the selling for him in return for an option to buy a controlling interest at net asset value in three years' time. It would even go so far as to find a finance company to help Marcus set up as a manufacturer. Marcus, being a courteous individual, thanked them and politely declined the offer.

In the meantime, Marcus has received two promising offers, one from an Italian company and one from Taiwan. A firm of commercial solicitors in London is negotiating on his behalf, and he has great hopes of a satisfactory arrangement being made.

Example 5.3: Turbotte Manufacturing Company (page 85)

The company got off to a good start. The Home Counties Bank agreed to the loan, and the company's organization and methods were working well. Galligaskin and Breeks were selling plenty of cues, production was going as expected, and staff training was proceeding satisfactorily.

However, after four months James Turbotte set off for the Antipodes on a marketing survey tour, and in the course of this he made a bad mistake. Infected by the enthusiasm displayed for his product by an Australian company, he signed a contract for a very large order of cues, the production of which his firm would find impossible to finance. His calculations (on the back of an envelope) of the production capacity required, when checked later, were not too far out. By making a big effort and paying considerable overtime, the company could meet the contract without undue disruption of other commitments; but when it came to the required working capital, it was obvious that the money would not be available as needed. James had been careless in agreeing the amount and length of credit the purchasers would be allowed.

Julian Watchman, the finance director, was furious, and on James's return to England a very stormy meeting of the directors took place. The company, which had been so successful so far, had reached the limits of its financial resources, and the bank could not, or would not, help. As a last resort, James tried to get the payment term of the Australian contract revised. The Australians, whom he had found so hospitable, turned out to be tough bargainers, and the extra discount that had to be given almost wiped out the profit on the order.

To tide the company over this bad patch, the directors agreed not to draw their salaries during the crucial months, and the firm has managed to survive. In fact, it now looks forward with renewed confidence to a prosperous future.

Postscript

In the previous pages I have described some of the necessary things a man or woman needs if he or she is setting out to run his or her own business. But there is one cardinal virtue that he or she must have: courage. If you fear too much, don't start your own business, or buy one from somebody else. Your place is in some safe bureaucracy.

One of the first jobs I was given by my firm, way back in 1946 just after the Second World War, was to go and see a middle-aged man who had been persuaded to buy a small chemist's shop. He had previously been a Co-op employee. I was sent to try to encourage him, and to emphasize the solid profitability of the shop he had bought. On his first day in his own shop I found him in a state of shivering collapse. A genial Irishman and I managed to get him through the day, but that night he took cyanide and died. His courage was just not up to the job of sole responsibility. He should have stayed in the safe refuge of the Co-op.

In my book Alexander Battersby, the joiner, and Dr K J Allan PhD, the entrepreneurial scientist, have one thing, at least, in common: they both have hearts stout enough to see them through.

The other thing they have in common with all self-employed people is their responsibility. I use the word in its true sense, in that they must answer for their deeds with their own well-being. If they succeed they get the reward; if they fail they pay for it personally. The buck stops with them. If Alexander Battersby is chosen by someone to do a job for them, that person will sign the cheque for the work done. There is not a civil servant, not in all Whitehall, even if he rise to the very top, that can say as much. I like to think that, when Alexander Battersby and Sir Humphrey Panjandrum GCMG appear together at the pearly gates where everything is known, that the jobbing joiner will be asked in first.

Where to go for further advice

If you were, say, the head of marketing in a large company, you would have colleagues. There would be not only a managing director, but also, in the nearby offices, a finance director, somebody responsible for production, and so on. You could concentrate on your own department's problems and let other people deal with everything else. For the sole owner of a small business, however, there is no one in the next office. You may well find such isolation and independence satisfying and even exhilarating. Many do. But it is likely that advice appropriate to your position will be hard to come by.

The government has made a considerable effort to set up advisory systems for small businesses, but inevitably this has tended to be the provision of specialized packages of advice on, for example, marketing, employment problems, bookkeeping and the like. Unfortunately, in the pool of available advisers, there is a scarcity of former managing directors and successful sole proprietors. The advisers are usually recruited from among specialists taking early retirement. This is not to denigrate their skill in advising, once a sound diagnosis has been made; but it is a fact that marketing experts tend to see problems as sales problems, bankers to see them in financial terms, and so on. Such specialized expertise may not be skilled in spotting the real underlying problems or in taking a balanced view of a company (see Chapter 9). The person running a small business, more often than not, needs help in asking the right questions before going to an expert for the answers.

Your accountant

Your accountant should be a person of experience and imagination who can help you to diagnose the real cause of any problems, or point you in the way of exploiting opportunities and suggest where you should go for other specialist advice.

It is often difficult to decide which accountant will serve you best. Don't just rely on the *Yellow Pages*. Have a word with other small businesses in your locality to find out what they ask for and get from their accountants – and how much they pay. Make sure, too, that the firm you choose does not hand you over to an inexperienced beginner. The small business needs experienced advice, and an accountant capable of giving such is well worth the fee.

Locally available advice

Enterprise agencies came into existence some 25 years ago as the result of local initiatives by business people and borough and county councils. Staffed by directors seconded from large firms and volunteer retired business people, they immediately filled a gap in the advisory services field, and still do so.

They have changed somewhat since the early days. There have been many local developments and name changes. In the previous chapters I have stuck to the term enterprise agency, as it was under that term that I worked for several happy, and I hope useful, years. But in many areas the name has been changed or the agency has been incorporated into a variety of 'one-stop' advisory services. But the advice goes on. Apply either to your local chamber of commerce or to your local authority for the name and address to contact.

The chamber of commerce

Do join your local chamber of commerce, if only for the contacts you can make. They can help you in many ways.

Your trade association

When you are doing your market research, it is often wise to get in touch with the trade association relevant to your business. It may provide useful statistics and other information, and enable you to decide whether there is sufficient potential to give you a chance of success. The local Chamber of Commerce will be able to supply the address.

Your local authority

Many county library services are very well organized to help the start-up business person. The local business libraries will prove to be a particularly useful source of information for your market research. Consult the librarian.

Your customers

Always talk to your customers. Do not hesitate to ask their advice (remembering, however, that their advice will not be unbiased). You will have consulted as many potential customers as possible in assessing the market for your product, and your business plan will be built on what they told you. Do not neglect them as a source of information and assistance later.

Your suppliers

A major supplier has a vested interest in the success of your business. Listen to the supplier's advice – unless it is trying to sell you something you don't really want. Remember, your supplier can be a valuable source of trade gossip and information about your competitors.

Appendices

Appendix 1: Help for small businesses

The following organizations are some of those that offer help of various sorts for small firms. If you are in any doubt as to how to get in touch with them, your local Business Link should be able to tell you.

Banks

Most banks publish free booklets on many aspects of starting and running a business, give away forms on which to do financial planning, and run newsletters.

British Overseas Trade Board

This government body, within the Department of Trade and Industry, gives leaflets, help and advice on exporting.

Chambers of commerce

Joining the local chamber can be a good way of making business contacts, as well as giving you access to a library and information service, help with exporting, and a voice in representations to public authorities.

Cooperative development agencies

These organizations give help and advice to people wishing to set up a cooperative venture.

County courts

They give away a booklet on making claims for payment of debts of up to £3,000, and what to do if such a claim is made against you.

Customs and Excise VAT offices

Their staff offer advice on all aspects of VAT and dispense free booklets (visit www.hmce.gov.uk).

Department of Employment

Advice and information on setting up and running a small firm, and useful free booklets.

Department of Trade and Industry

This government department is the main source of grants for industry. Its regional offices can advise on every facet of their help (visit www.dti.gov.uk).

Development agencies (for Scotland, Wales and Northern Ireland)

These are government bodies that can offer a wide range of advice, help, premises and funds for business.

Enterprise agencies

These partnerships between the public and private sectors aim to offer advice, help and other facilities to encourage new and existing businesses.

Highlands and Islands Enterprise

This northern Scottish organization supports, helps and promotes small businesses in its area.

Industrial training boards

Although many have been abolished or changed in nature in the past few years, some offer excellent publications to help new and small firms in their particular industry.

HM Revenue & Customs Inspectors of Taxes

Leaflets and advice are given on the tax position of businesses, which can be most useful to new starters (visit www.hmrc.gov.uk).

Jobcentres

Not only are they a source of recruitment, Jobcentres also carry a stock of leaflets and Department of Employment publications, many of which are essential reading for an employer. See www.jobcentreplus.gov.uk.

Learning and skills councils

The Learning and Skills Council and the network of local learning and skills councils replaced training and enterprise councils (TECs) in 2001. Their role is to find training and workforce development in England, with a budget of some

£5 billion. See www.lsc.gov.uk   The enterprise role of the former TECs has been taken forward by the DTI's Small Business Service.

Local authorities

They can usually provide information on any industrial aid that may be available locally. In addition, as one of the most influential enforcement bodies acting on small firms, they can advise you on how to avoid trouble. The main contacts are the planning department, health inspectors, fire department, building inspectors and trading standards offices.

Mid-Wales Development Board

This is a government body which offers help to small firms in rural Wales.

Newspaper Publishers Association

This body lays down the rules governing, among other things, mail-order advertising in most newspapers and magazines. Anyone planning to sell by this method should contact it well in advance of trying to advertise.

Patent Office

The Patent Office offers an informative set of leaflets on its concerns.

Royal Mail

The Royal Mail (www.royalmail.com) gives considerable concessions to volume users of its services in general, and especially to first-time users of direct-mail selling. Postal sales representatives at head post offices provide the details.

Tourist boards

Organized on a regional basis, the tourist boards offer management advice, publicity and grants for tourism-based enterprises. These do not have to be just hotels: they are concerned to help most firms having some tourism aspect to their operations. They also publish some useful guides to running different sorts of tourism businesses.

Appendix 2: Useful names, addresses and websites

Advisory, Conciliation and Arbitration Service (ACAS)
Head Office, Brandon House
180 Borough High Street
London SE1 1LW
Tel: 020 7210 3613
www.acas.org.uk

Agricultural Development Advisory Service (ADAS)
Woodthorne, Wergs Road
Wolverhampton WV6 8TQ
Tel: 0845 766 0085
Email: enquiries@adas.co.uk
www.adas.co.uk

Alliance of Small Firms and Self Employed People
33 The Green
Calne, Wiltshire SN11 8DJ
Tel: 01249 817003

BBC External Services
PO Box 76, Bush House
Strand, London WC2B 4PU
Tel: 020 7240 3456

British Franchise Association
Franchise Chambers, Thames View
Newtown Road, Henley-on-Thames
Oxfordshire RG9 1HG
Tel: 01491 578050
www.thebfa.org.uk

British Institute of Management Small Firms Information Service
Management House, Cottingham Road
Corby, Northamptonshire NN17 1TT
Tel: 01536 20422

British Insurance Brokers Association
BIBA House, 14 Bevis Marks
London EC3N 7AT
Tel: 020 7623 9043
www.biba.org.uk

British Overseas Trade Board
1 Victoria Street
London SW1H 0ET
Tel: 020 7215 7877

British Standards Institution
389 Chiswick High Road
London W4 4AJ
Tel: 020 8996 9001
www.bsi-global.com

British Technology Group
101 Newington Causeway
London SE1 6BU
Tel: 020 7403 6666

Building Research Establishment
Bucknalls Lane, Garston
Watford WD25 9XX
Tel: 01923 664000
Fax: 01923 664010
Email: enquiries@bre.co.uk
www.bre.co.uk
and
Kelvin Road
East Kilbride
Glasgow G75 0RZ
Tel: 01355 576200
Email: eastkilbride@bre.co.uk

Business Link
Tel: 0845 600 9006
www.businesslink.gov.uk

Central Office of Information
Hercules Road
London SE1 7DU
Tel: 020 7928 2345
www.coi.gov.uk

Chartered Institute of Marketing
Moor Hall, Cookham
Maidenhead SL6 9QH
Tel: 01628 427500
www.cim.co.uk

Chartered Institute of Patent Attorneys
95 Chancery Lane
London WC2A 1DT
Tel: 020 7405 9450
Fax: 020 7430 0471
Email: mail@cipa.org.uk
www.cipa.org.uk

Companies Registration Offices:

Companies House
Crown Way
Maindy
Cardiff CF14 3UZ
Tel: 0870 3333636

Companies House
21 Bloomsbury Street
London WC1B 3XD
Tel: 0870 3333636

Companies House
37 Castle Terrace
Edinburgh EH1 2EB
Tel: 0870 3333636

Department of Commerce
64 Chichester Street
Belfast BT1 4JX
Tel: 02890 234488

Cooperative Development Agency
Broadmead House, 21 Panton Street
London SW1Y 4DR
Tel: 020 7839 2988

Country Land and Business Association
16 Belgrave Square
London SW1X 8PQ
Tel: 020 7235 0511
www.cla.org.uk

Crafts Council
44a Pentonville Road
London NI 9BY
Tel: 020 7278 7700
www.craftscouncil.org.uk

Department for Environment, Food and Rural Affairs
Nobel House, 17 Smith Square
London SW1P 3JR
Tel: 0845 9335577
(for free booklets on planning permission see next entry)

Department for Business, Enterprise and Regulatory Reform
1 Victoria Street
London SW1H 0ET
Tel: 020 7215 5000
Email: enquiries@berr.gsi.gov.uk

Design Council
34 Bow Street
London WC2E 7DL
Tel: 020 7420 5200

Durham University Business School
Mill Hill Lane
Durham DH1 3LB
Tel: 0191 334 5200
www.dur.ac.uk/dbs

Equipment Leasing Association
18 Upper Grosvenor Street
London W1X 9PB
Tel: 020 7491 2783

Export Credits Guarantee Department
PO Box 2200, 2 Exchange Tower
Harbour Exchange Square
London E14 9GS
Tel: 020 7512 7000
www.ecgd.gov.uk

Finance Houses Association
18 Upper Grosvenor Street
London W1X 9PB
Tel: 020 7491 2783

Greater London Enterprise (GLE)
New City Court, 20 St Thomas Street
London SE1 9RS
Tel: 020 7403 0300
Fax: 020 7403 1742
Email: info@gle.co.uk
www.gle.co.uk

Highlands and Islands Enterprise
Cowan House, Inverness Business Park
Inverness IV2 7GF
Tel: 01463 234171

Hotel Catering and Institutional Management Association
191 Trinity Road
London SW17 7HN
Tel: 020 8672 4251

Industrial and Commercial Finance Corporation (3i)
16 Palace Street
London SW1E 5JD
Tel: 020 7928 3131
www.3i.com

Intellectual Property Office
Concept House, Cardiff Road
Newport, South Wales NP10 8QQ
Tel: 01633 813930

IT for All
2,000 centres across the UK
Tel: 0800 456 567
www.iclc.org.uk

Institute of Directors
116 Pall Mall
London SW1Y 5ED
Tel: 020 7839 1233

Institute of Patentees and Inventors
PO Box 39296
London SE3 7WH
Tel: 0871 226 2091
www.invent.org.uk

Institute of Trade Mark Attorneys
Canterbury House, 4th Floor
2–6 Sydenham Road
Croydon CR0 9XE
Tel: 020 8686 2052
www.itma.org.uk

Livewire
Loan Guarantee Scheme
Design Works Unit 15
William Street, Felling
Gateshead NE10 0JP
Tel: 0845 757 3252
www.shell-livewire.org

Manufacturers' Agents' Association of Great Britain and Ireland Incorporated
(MAA)
Unit 16, Thrales End
Harpenden, Herts AL5 3NS
Tel: 01582 766092
E-mail: info@themaa.co.uk
Website: www.themaa.co.uk

MOPS (Mail Order Protection Scheme)
see The National Newspapers' Mail Order Protection Scheme Ltd

National Business Angels Network
Website: www.nationalbusangels.co.uk

National Computing Centre Ltd
Oxford Road
Manchester M1 7ED
Tel: 0161 242 2121

National Farmers' Union
Agriculture House, Steneleigh Park
Stoneleigh, Warwickshire CV8 2TZ
Tel: 024 7685 8500
www.nfuonline.com

National Federation of Self-Employed and Small Businesses
Sir Frank Whittle Way
Blackpool Business Park
Blackpool FY4 2FE
Tel: 01253 336000
www.fsb.org.uk

National Newspapers' Safe Home Ordering Protection Scheme
18a King Street
Maidenhead SL6 1EF
Tel: 01628 641930

Newspaper Publishers Association (NPA)
8th Floor, St Andrews House
18–20 St Andrew Street
London EC4A 3AY
Tel: 020 7636 7014
Fax: 020 7631 5119

The Patent Office
Concept House, Cardiff Road
Newport, South Wales NP10 8QQ
Tel: 0845 9500505

Prince's Trust
Tel: 0800 842 842 (freephone)
www.princes-trust.org.uk

Production Engineering Research Association (PERA)
Melton Mowbray
Leicestershire LE13 0PB
Tel: 01664 64133

Scottish Enterprise
5 Atlantic Quay
150 Broomielaw
Glasgow G2 8LU
Tel: 0141 248 2700

Small Business Bureau
Curzon House, Church Road
Windlesham
Surrey GU20 6BH
Tel: 01276 452020
www.smallbusinessbureau.org.uk

Union of Independent Companies
9 Pelham Place
London SW7 2NQ
Tel: 020 7225 0444

Venture Capital Report
www.vcrdirectory.co.uk

More useful websites

Some of these sites have already been listed earlier in this Appendix. They are listed separately here for ease of use by people with web connections. The list isn't meant to be comprehensive, but it does contain some of those most useful to a small firm. A couple of evenings spent surfing websites that seem of most interest should expose quite a few that are worth bookmarking, as well as yielding some information of more immediate interest.

Advisory, Conciliation and Arbitration Service	www.acas.org.uk
Agricultural Development and Advisory Service	www.adas.co.uk
British Employment Law	www.emplaw.co.uk
British Franchise Association	www.thebfa.org
British Standards Institution	www.bsi-global.com
British Tourist Authority	www.visitbritain.com
Business Link	www.businesslink.org
Companies House	www.companieshouse.gov.uk
Confederation of British Industry	www.cbi.org.uk
Department for Business Enterprise and Regulatory Reform	www.berr.gov.uk
Department for Education and Skills	www.dfes.gov.uk
Export Credit Guarantee Department	www.ecgd.gov.uk
Government search site	www.open.gov.uk
HM Revenue and Customs	www.hmrc.gov.uk
Information Commissioner's Office	www.ico.gov.uk
Intellectual Property Office	www.ipo.gov.uk
Learning and Skills Council	www.lsc.gov.uk
LiveWire	www.shell-livewire.com
MINTEL Research	www.mintel.com
National Federation of Enterprise Agencies	www.nfea.com
Office of National Statistics	www.statistics.gov.uk
Prince's Trust	www.princes-trust.org.uk
Sales agents	www.sales-agents.com
Scottish Enterprise	www.scottish-enterprise.com
Small Business Service	www.sbs.gov.uk

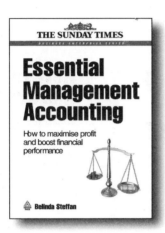